# FEEL, DEAL & HEAL

D1613186

## NIRMAL YADAV

FP LIFE

Published by

**FiNGER**PRINT! **L!FE**

An imprint of Prakash Books India Pvt. Ltd.

113/A, Darya Ganj, New Delhi-110 002,
Tel: (011) 2324 7062 – 65, Fax: (011) 2324 6975
E-mail: info@prakashbooks.com/sales@prakashbooks.com

facebook www.facebook.com/fingerprintpublishing
twitter www.twitter.com/FingerprintP, www.fingerprintpublishing.com

Copyright © 2017 Prakash Books India Pvt. Ltd.
Copyright Text © Nirmal Yadav

All rights reserved. No part of this publication may be reproduced, stored in a retrieval system or transmitted in any form or by any means, electronic, mechanical, photocopying, recording or otherwise (except for mentions in reviews or edited excerpts in the media) without the written permission of the publisher.

ISBN: 978 81 7599 445 4

Processed & printed in India

Daughter of a newspaper publisher, life comes full circle for author Nirmal Yadav as her book goes into print.

Born in a small town of Haryana, Nirmal married a soldier at the age of twenty-one and signed up for three decades of a nomadic life— living, learning, and unlearning, all around the country, eventually with two kids in tow. While her husband led a regiment, she chose to lead a classroom and spent many years teaching.

Finding herself in the predicament of no longer anchoring her family's life, her children having grown up and gone, she took a courageous leap towards a new career. She trained as a psychotherapist and rediscovered herself while helping others in turmoil.

Incidentally, Nirmal got into the 10m Air Pistol shooting sport, two years back. She not only won a gold medal in the 10m Air Pistol Championship Veterans Women's category at the 60th National Shooting Championship 2016 held in Pune, but she also set a record.

Nirmal has spent a good part of her life working at various social service organizations. This book is a collection of life lessons and hard-earned wisdom and it promises to be a reliable companion at every stage of life.

# Contents

# DEDICATION

TO MY MOTHER, THE WARRIOR

# ACKNOWLEDGEMENTS

I express my gratitude to all the wonderful authors I have read over the last few years. They have been my inspiration. And to all the people around me who have helped me get the perspective I am trying to communicate today, thank you.

# Preface

I belong to the older generation when all the decisions were made by our parents. And we, as children, had hardly any say, even in the immensely personal matters like choosing a career or a life partner. Our consent was not considered necessary. Our parents knew better, we assumed. Flouting parental authority was unheard of.

So, I married the man my parents chose for me. Every marriage needs work, so did mine. During my stint as an Army officer's wife, I was dabbling with enhancing my education too. And as if this was not enough, suddenly, I had two strangers to handle. I did not know when my two little kids grew up into rebellious teenagers. It was the most confusing, difficult, and testing phase of my life. Everything seemed to happen without me having a say in the direction it took.

It was too much for me to handle with absolutely no one to help. The more I tried to take control of things, the more they seemed to slip away. I was desperately trying to seek answers to some questions. I was at my lowest ebb. I did not want to live like this for ever. I knew I had to do something about it. It was during this phase that I did a lot of reading and soul searching. I worked with various social organizations, studied psychotherapy, which I experimented on myself and the people around me. Somewhere along the way, I realized how ignorant I had been! My plight was that of the foolish King who was planning to cover his entire kingdom with cowhide because his feet hurt when he walked about. It was his court jester who suggested him to put a piece of cowhide under his own feet. I needed to do exactly that—bring a change in myself rather than trying to change the world. I had to work on myself. I needed to grow. And, I did. I got introduced to a new me. I loved it.

I can proudly claim today that this book is the result of some the choices I have made in the near and distant past. Some decisions were harder than others. Resigning from a comfortable and permanent Central School job was one tough choice. I felt there was very little scope for my own personal growth in that profession. I did a lot of complaining in the beginning but did nothing to change, till it finally dawned on me that I had to stop prolonging my misery and needed to act. I stopped all the complaining and resigned from my job. I was happy to get more time to do what I wanted to do. I started making conscious choices on a daily basis. I did not yield to the temptations of getting into inconsequential indulgences like gossip or getting glued to the TV. I chose to spend time in more enriching and constructive activities like reading, conducting workshops, and helping emotionally and mentally-disturbed people. Being in the company of like-minded people helped a lot. One thing led to another and soon these new experiences brought out the best in me. I finally got what I had been yearning for, for so long—'TRUE HAPPINESS.' It has been a beautiful journey, and as I continue to tread on my chosen path, I am delighted by every bit of experience that comes my way.

We still do not have answers to some age-old questions: Why is the world the way it is, where do we come from, the meaning of life and death, life after death, rebirth, heaven and hell, and so on. Mankind has pondered over the same mysteries since time immemorial. But today, I have the answer to maybe the biggest question of them all, 'Why are our souls trapped in an unhappy mind and an unhappy body?'

This book is a compilation of my thoughts on how to be happy and how to live our life at its best, no matter what the circumstances. The book is for all those who are ready for an inner transformation and are willing to grow. Here you will find inspiring words to keep you hungry for more, as you put in the effort to reach a level where you become capable of breaking out of collected mind patterns that have been keeping us in bondage to suffering since ages. And even if you are not ready to live and practice it yet, it will give a new dimension to your thinking. A new seed which sown now, may grow within you till you are ready to sit under its shade and reap the fruit of your labour. To me, even if it succeeds in making a difference to a few lives, this book has been well worth writing.

I would like to share with you, dear reader, a story narrated to me by my father. Early morning one day, a young man was walking on the beach enjoying the beauty of sunrise. He suddenly noticed a shadow dancing in the distance. When he moved closer, he realized it was an old man who was not dancing but picking up starfish from the beach and throwing them in the water one by one. He asked the old man why he was doing that. "If they stay out of water after sunrise, they will die," replied the old man. "I don't believe it is worth it! The beach is so long and the starfishes are in thousands. What you are doing can hardly make a difference!" the young man sounded amused. The old man picked another starfish, tossed it into the waves, and smiled, "It makes a difference to this one," he said.

Thousands of candles can be lighted from a single candle. If not many, I am sure this book will change the lives of at least a few, and those few will in turn change a few more lives, and hopefully this circle will go on and on and on . . .

Read this book slowly, as you would read a story to a child. Take one chapter at a time and ponder over it for a couple of hours. Keep reading it, until you absorb all the wisdom. If you are not happy, the first step is to find out what makes you unhappy. Take a long thoughtful look at what you are doing at this point of time. There has to be something wrong with that. Pause for a moment. Apply your will and make a conscious effort to experiment with different choices till you get the desired result. Apply some of the skills mentioned in this book in your daily life and eventually they will become a way of life.

See yourself and the world around you changing. Hear yourself saying, "Life is beautiful!"

What do each of us want?

What are our objects of desire?

What are our subjects of desire?

The answers may vary from person to person. Some people want to be successful; some want money. Some want to get knowledge; some want a spellbound audience for their creativity. Some crave for glamour; some for fame. Some want to rule others; some want to be humble persons at the feet of God. Some may want something else not mentioned here. And there may be some who wish to achieve a combination of all these things, in varying intensities. The dynamic behind our longings and cravings is that we all want to feel happy and fulfilled. No doubt about it. No two opinions. The ways and means might differ—through money, knowledge, beauty, power, fame, glamour, love, passion, etc.; the list is endless. The techniques used to be happy could be different. But it is the universal need of every human—To Be Happy!

The whole world has been continuously seeking for this rare commodity. The market assures us that happiness can be bought.

People go happiness shopping. So what if it comes at a hefty price! But do we even have any inkling about what makes us happy? Are we really happy when those desired moments of achievement come? And how long do those moments last? Do we remember how many moments of happiness we had last week, last month or last year? If you feel lost and confused, rest assure, somewhere, something is wrong. Maurice Sendak said, "There must be more to life than having everything." May be we are on the wrong track. May be we are carrying a wrong map. May be we are looking for happiness in all the wrong places. May be we need a different take on happiness all together.

Shakespeare said, "sometimes there is a method in madness." For happiness, there has to be a method too. Let us strive to adopt a simpler, less expensive and less time-consuming method. Here is a fundamental solution which strikes at the very root of the problem instead of merely papering over the cracks.

To attain happiness we need to know:

- The influences and factors responsible for taking us away from happiness. Tackle each specific cause.
- The unexploited assets, skills and techniques that can bring us closer to happiness. Enhance them.
- There are some of the important and difficult phases in life where we have no choice but to face them squarely. Deal with them skilfully.

# PART ONE

# Happiness Preamble

In a book published before his election, Benedict XVI refers to a Buddhist parable.

A king in northern India once got bored and gathered a number of blind men who did not know what an elephant was. He had some of the blind men touch the head of the elephant and said, "This is an elephant." He said the same thing to the others as he asked them to touch the trunk, or the ears, or the feet, or the hair at the end of the elephant's tail. Then the king asked the blind men what an elephant was, and each gave a different explanation depending on the part he had been permitted to touch. The blind men began to argue, and the argument became violent, until a fist fight broke out among them, which provided much entertainment to the king.

Just like the blind men, we humans are unable to comprehend true happiness. We have no idea of what happiness truly is and how to nurture it. The moment we think we have got hold of the tail, we are off again.

What has gone wrong? Why do we keep missing the point? Is it simply impossible to achieve happiness? Or is it that it is not where we have been looking for it? I agree with the latter. Happiness is the easiest and the simplest thing to be attained. It's just that we are all carrying a wrong map. We are looking for happiness in all the wrong places.

Let's elaborate this further.

## A distorted view

We all suffer from faulty beliefs and thinking habits that cause us mental turmoil and unhappiness. We have developed a wrong idea of what constitutes true happiness. We think:

### Happiness Comes Through External Sources

For centuries we humans have been living with the misconception that happiness is working hard, earning money, building a bank balance, and buying expensive things. We think, "If only I lived in this bungalow, became the President of some great company, married a more understanding woman, moved to Mumbai, bought a BMW, I'd be happy." We try to manipulate conditions so as to experience things our way. So we all slog for twelve hours a day, depriving ourselves of the little pleasures of life. We keep on desiring incessantly. We do not enjoy what we have, but want what we don't have. We always have IFS and BUTS. I know I have this, but . . . The process never ends. This is why, we have more 'things' and more 'comfort' than any other civilization in history, yet depression and unhappiness are probably more widespread today than in any other times.

Bangalore-based guru Rishi Prabhakar argues, "If it was true that happiness lies in an object, more of that object would bring more happiness. If sugar makes you happy, then more sugar should make you even happier." What we need to understand is that this is just momentary, situational happiness—not true happiness. Chasing desires is like a dog chasing his tail. Result? Only circles, no forward progress.

Osho, one of the new age gurus once narrated this story:

A man once visited a madhouse. The doctor was taking him round the wards. They came to a cage. A man was beating his head, pulling his hair, crying, and holding a small picture near his chest. It was pathetic. The visitor asked, "What has happened to this unfortunate man?" The doctor said, "He could not marry the woman he loved. She decided to marry somebody else. Since then he has lost his sanity. He carries her picture all the time—day, night, awake, asleep—and he is in deep anguish. His misery is immense."

> Chasing desires is like a dog chasing his tail. Result? Only circles, no forward progress.

They came to another cage, opposite the first one. Another person was raving mad, hitting his head against the walls, fighting with some shadows. He looked like a murderer. And the visitor asked, "What has happened to this man?" The doctor started laughing, "That woman married this man! See what has happened to him!"

There are many contradictions in life like this. A poor man wants riches; a rich man loses sleep over his riches. A short person wants to become tall; a tall person develops a hunch in an attempt to look short. Some yearn for fame; famous ones envy the freedom of a common man. Our restless minds make us jump from one ambition to another. The quest is never ending. We let it enslave us till our physical and mental faculties break down.

There is a lady in my neighbourhood, perpetually unhappy and miserable. She has a loving husband and two wonderful sons. She is doing very well in her career and earns more than many. One day she was detected with a tumour which was operated upon successfully. Any other person would have heaved a sigh of relief and thanked

God for giving a second life. But that was not the case with her. Rather than being happy, she was highly upset, for it had cost her a few days of her salary. It seems that we have conditioned ourselves to be miserable.

It is not the external situations that are the reasons for anybody's happiness or unhappiness. If it was so, we would not have been sad for nothing at times. On such days every person we meet is rude and uncooperative. It seems the whole world is conspiring against us. And sometimes if we are happy, we are positive to all negative things or situations. Actually, it is our mind that co-creates our experiences.

## Outer Beauty Brings Happiness

'Look good and feel good' is the sole outlook of today's modern world. Everyone is trying to be a fitness freak. The surge of beauty products and cosmetic operations in the market has increased with the number of people wanting to become slim and beautiful. On my daily evening walks, I am shocked to overhear children not more than ten years discussing their figure and weight and exchanging notes on parlours, gyms, and cosmetic surgeries. Some fads take a toll on our lives. For instance, the trend of healthy lifestyles is becoming unhealthier. People are going to extremes. Look at what the young girls are doing to become beauty queens! Some are so obsessed with calorie counts, nutrition, and organic food that they have actually forgotten the real taste of food and eat only to vomit it out. We are falling victims to physical and mental ailments, which were not known in old times. Parents need to help their children to identify what is healthy and unhealthy for them.

Physical and mental health is interrelated. The mental health strongly affects our physical health. If emotions are not handled and released rightly and wisely, they solidify by causing muscle contractions. This in turn blocks the flow of energy and weakens the immune system.

Ignored mental health hampers healthy growth, sours attitude, and tears apart relationships. If we are in harmony, mentally and physically, things will be under our control.

Unfortunately, the time children and parents should be spending on inculcating good values, is being spent on enhancing outer beauty. We have not been taught how to deal with mental pollution. We live through with fractured minds. At such times we need to rework our feelings.

> A happy person is happy for no reason. Such a person does not draw happiness from everyday experiences; he rather brings happiness to his experiences.

### The Belief We Are Living an Intentional Life

Another clearly mistaken belief is that we are being the masters of our own lives and doing our best to live a happy and fulfilled life. We hold external factors responsible for all the wrong things that happen in our lives, not realizing that we are making ourselves slaves of circumstances. Most of us end up spending our entire life reacting to life events. We let others run our lives, instead of the other way around. As Dexter Yager says, "The average person's life consists of twenty years of having parents ask them where he is going, forty years of having a spouse ask the same question, and finally, in the end, the mourner wonders the same thing."

People know how to drive a car and keep it in control. They know how and when to change gears, slow down, speed up, or use the brake. They push their luck and try to control others, but fail to be their own masters. They live life by chance, not by choice. It is, therefore, not surprising that people are feeling stressed out. Living an intentional life is to make life happen, not let life happen. Living with intention means bringing into our lives what we want to, deliberately and by choice.

So it is not what happens to us that creates misery. Happiness needs no reason. Happiness needs no manipulation. A happy person is happy for no reason. Such a person does not draw happiness from everyday experiences; he rather brings happiness to his experiences. It is our lack of courage to deal with misfortunes that makes us choose an easy way out by blaming it on luck and destiny. Once we let go of this attitude, we can feel, deal, and heal our emotions and hop on the path of happiness we have been craving for long—a deep, permanent, and value-based happiness. We can easily overcome our imaginary fears just by changing our thinking pattern.

# Romancing With New Discovery

A soldier in a remote camp returned to his billet after a day's march under the broiling sun.

"What a life!" said one new soldier, "Miles from anywhere, a sergeant who thinks he's Attila the Hun, no women, no booze, no leave—and to top it all, my boots are two sizes small."

"You don't want to put up with that, chum," said his neighbour. "Why don't you go in for another pair?"

"Not likely," pat came the reply. "Taking them off is the only pleasure I've got!" (*Joy* by Osho)

Deep down in our minds we have become victims of false beliefs and erroneous thoughts. We have our opinions, concepts, expectations locked in our mental box and we try to hold on to them for ever. We have become so addicted to them that we have accepted them as a part of our personality. We resist any change because it's much too risky. We prefer to live a life of ouches and grouches than to do something about it.

To deny any change means to deny growing. And without growth, the life within starts to stink and disintegrate. We cannot keep going round the mulberry bush and expect different results. The layers of old habits and false beliefs are like the onion skins that need to be peeled off if we want happiness to be at our doorstep.

> The happy people are not those who have the best of everything in life, but those who make the most of what life hands over to them.

## So what things do we need to do differently to go from surviving to thriving?

Up until now, we might have been allowing life to work us instead of we working life. We do not have to be just an actor, living the script given to us by somebody else, anymore. We can be our own writer, producer, and director. There is no need to rely on others to make us happy. What we really need to do is to release the hidden handbrakes that stop us from moving forward in life. We need a paradigm shift—a change from one way of thinking to another. It applies to anything on earth—our job, our married life, our relationships, our home, our surroundings, and more importantly, our health. We need to let go of the old ideas and values that do not go with the change that is taking place at a rapid pace and replace them with the new ones. Otherwise our condition will be like that of a miserable child who has outgrown his shoes, but has not been given better fitting ones. How much of it do we recognize, internalize, or apply, depends on the intensity of our desire to change. And this in turn will decide our happiness quotient.

Fall in love with yourself. Untill you learn to feel, deal, and heal, you cannot fathom how it feels to be in complete control. The happy people are not those who have the best of everything in life, but those who make the most of what life hands over to them. Important ingredients or components required to live an intentional life—the essence of living a purposefully achieved happy life, are taken in detail in the following chapters. The thing to understand is that each component is the part of a woven fabric of living an intentional life. We have to get to the root cause to fight the problem. In order to achieve happiness, we simply need to answer these 3 questions:

What do I need to STOP doing?

What do I need to START doing?

What do I need to DO MORE OF?

We need some techniques to tackle the emotional barriers that we have created for ourselves before they exhaust us like a bottomless pit. However, since the disturbing attitudes and negative emotions are based on misconceptions, they can be eliminated through cultivating realistic views and constructive emotions. Emotional Analysis is a useful starting point for understanding our own emotions, as well as those of others. It helps us to get in tune with our emotions. It makes it easier for us to understand the dark emotional areas of our life, which in turn helps us to step out of our deep, pervasive negative thoughts and moods. We can benefit by using them as an 'early-warning bell' and turn them around to overcome unhappiness.

Albert Einstein has rightly said, "Sometimes one pays most for the things one gets for nothing." In the following chapters, we will discuss the deep rooted common energy zappers in our mental habits—roadblocks to happiness. We need to search and fix them out.

" The first step in seeking happiness is learning. We first have to learn how negative emotions and behaviours are harmful to us and how positive emotions are helpful. We must also realize that these negative emotions are not only very bad and harmful to one personally, but are also harmful to society and the future of the whole world. "

**(Dalai Lama)**

# Roadblocks To Happiness

"What we focus on, we empower and enlarge. Good multiplies when focused upon. Negativity multiplies when focused upon. The choice is ours: Which do we want more of?"

(Julia Cameron, *Blessings*)

## Negative Thinking

Once it so happened that my elder sister had a glass of milk for breakfast. After about an hour, while pouring milk for me, she saw a long piece of brown thread in the milk. She mistook it for a lizard and remembered having drunk the same milk. She got so paranoid just thinking about it that she started feeling giddy and nauseous. She started howling and fainted with the fear of dying. Though it embarrassed her no end when she was told that it was not a lizard but merely a piece of thread, it's been ages since she drank milk.

Incidents like these prove that there is a relation between the mind and the body. Our body reacts positively to positive thoughts and negatively to negative thoughts. While the power of positive thinking works wonders, so does the power of negativity. It manifests itself through fear, inferiority complex, excessive self-criticism, and pessimism. Such an attitude damages one's confidence, reduces performance levels, and even paralyzes mental ability as it happened with my sister.

Negative thinking is as pervasive as the common cold, but far more damaging. And it does not go away so easily. It cripples and corrodes the confidence level of the person suffering from it. It's like a hole in the pitcher—dripping away our confidence and self-esteem. We can hardly use our mental faculties appropriately. Our thinking pattern is flawed. Constant negative thoughts release toxins and cloud the rational mind which results in affecting our physical health and performance in every sphere of life. The constant stress that flows from a negative attitude saps one's energy, focus, and motivation. Blinded by our own negativity, we prevent ourselves from seeing the good around us. Here is a Yiddish folk tale:

An old man sat outside the walls of a great city.

When travellers approached, they asked the old man, "What kind of people live in this city?"

And the old man answered, "What kind of people live in the place where you come from?"

If the travellers answered, "Only bad people live in the place where we come from," the old man would reply, "Continue, you will find only bad people here." But if the travellers answered, "Good people live in the place where we come from," then the old man would say, "Enter, for here, too, you will find only good people."

> The constant stress that flows from a negative attitude saps one's energy, focus, and motivation.

One more thing about the negative thinker is that he wishes the world to behave according to his wishes. When things don't work his way, he becomes an unhappy soul. Such a poisonous attitude prevents him from growing and learning—a must to cope with life's new challenges. He never changes, so he never grows, and drags through life as a miserable human being.

Habitual negativity makes one addicted to unhappiness in mind, body, and soul. A rotten attitude delays what one wants to get.

# De-conditioning the Thinking Pattern:

So how do we inoculate ourselves against such a harmful emotion? We all have a choice of producing positive or negative thoughts and actions. But there are some die-hard negative thinkers who believe that nothing on earth can change them. They are stubborn and rigid in their thoughts. It is almost like saying 'an old dog cannot be taught new tricks.' But then there is a huge difference between a dog and a human being. Human beings can have a change of heart and mind. Some bother, some ignore, some are blind to the fact that it is the little things in life that make us happy. Watching a rainbow appear on the clear blue sky after a rainy day beats any expensive oil painting by world famous artists. Watching a newborn baby yawn elicits more positive emotions than the labour that the mother goes through while giving birth. A husband's cleaning drive one Sunday at home creates far more happiness than his constant bickering nature.

Remember, as adults, we have the capability to unlearn and unleash the limiting beliefs and images that we have formed since childhood. If you seem to have trapped yourself to stay put at a comfort zone, you can change your comfort zone over time by making it your personal belief.

- **Recognize some of the gnawing drawbacks in thinking**

  In response to a professional setback, some will resign even before they start, "I can't finish this workout." "I can't lose weight." "I'll be last again." Do you find yourself putting yourself down? If yes, it's a wake-up call. This destructive habit is often a self-fulfilling prophecy. We talk ourselves out of improving our performance or developing good new habits. We talk ourselves into just giving up.

The subconscious mind is like the computer. What we feed in comes out. So if we feed into the computer, 'I am useless. No one likes me. I am a failure,' what do you think will the printer print? Don't expect the printer to come up with, 'Hi beautiful, sunshine of my life.' Likewise, what we put in our subconscious mind, results in the corresponding thoughts and actions.

Negative characters (villains of the real world) do not look devilish like Lucifer or conniving like Chanakya. They are within the family (are you thinking of your moralistic elder sister, or strict father, or orthodox aunty?) Do they begin their sentences with No, not possible? Even pesky, old neighbours or those with attitude can be included in this list. Psychiatrist, Daniel G Amen, calls such limiting thoughts that go on in the mind as ANTS (automatic negative thoughts.) Just as ants can ruin our picnic in the garden, the ANTS in our mind can ruin our experiences of life. Some call them 'inner critics.' Most negative thinkers become so when they are constantly expecting failure, or have self-doubts about their capabilities.

> A negative thinker wishes the world to behave according to his wishes. When things don't work his way, he becomes an unhappy soul.

The good news is that you have a chance to change it all and have a new improved lifestyle. Since everything starts with a thought, it would be wonderful to train the mind to be positive. Identify the crippling thoughts, flush them out, or change them. Do not worry. This doesn't require a sensational, criminal investigation trip. But, nonetheless, figure out those gloomy geeks who ruin an adventure (also pet projects, run down great ideas) by their pessimistic views. Here are some of the common types of automatic negative thoughts we need to be aware of:

i. **Overgeneralization**

Phrases like "I'll never become a doctor," "My mother is always critical of me," could be self-defeating. Words like 'never' and 'always' come from a general conclusion based on a single event. Keep a watch on such generalized negative thoughts. Try replacing them with "If I work hard, I have a fair chance of becoming a doctor." "Sometimes my mother bullies me. Let me find out what is upsetting about me."

ii. **Catastrophic Predicting**

The thoughts of some people start with the chances of disaster they over anticipate. Those who think, "Everyone will laugh at me if I participate in Indian Idol," however much talented they are, lose even before the competition begins. Winners are those who think positive—"You never know. I might win. After all, it's the first time for each one of us."

iii. **Mind Reading**

It means making assumptions about other people's thoughts and feelings without checking the evidence. "I am sure that the selection committee thinks I was stupid in the interview." Don't become a mind reader. You hardly know what is happening in your mind— let alone in other people's minds. Try replacing your negative thoughts by "Let me wait for the result to know what they thought of my performance."

iv. **Using 'should' and 'must' thoughts**

Those who use should or must thoughts for them or others, set themselves up for frustration. They end up feeling guilty at the end of the day. Instead of saying, "I must finish this project today," say, "I plan to or I intend to finish this project today."

v. **Personalizing**

Thinking about what someone said or didn't say or did or didn't do as some kind of reaction, is a way of personalizing things. "She didn't say hello to me. Obviously, she doesn't like me." Chances are that she didn't even see you.

vi. **Labelling**

When instead of saying "I made a mistake," you say, "I'm a complete loser," you are labelling yourself a fool, a failure. Labelling, when applied to other people, unfairly generalizes the other person in a derogatory way. For example, "My sister is an idiot." These labels are just abstractions that make people feel bad about themselves or others. As a result, their self-esteem takes a nose dive. There are a number of such negative sentences we utter or that have been residing in our subconscious mind for many years (in some cases many lifetimes).

Automatic Negative Thoughts often get started with intense emotional experiences from childhood or adolescence. Though the information from the past can be valuable, the key to resolve them lies primarily in the present.

Thoughts are like water currents that cannot be

stopped from meandering in the mind. But the course can be adjusted or altered for sure by using some techniques.

- **Use Thought-Awareness Method**

No amount of avoidance or positive self-talk will help till we are aware of negative self-talk. Avoiding thoughts consciously, might actually result in our thinking it all the more. In some of the experiments conducted by Daniel M Wegner of Trinity University in San Antonio, Texas, his subjects were asked to try not to think about a white bear. When they were asked to speak whatever came to their mind, most of them said 'white bears.'

A good method to fight out the problem is to bring awareness to the automatic negative thoughts we are indulged in. This will help us to be specific and realistic in our approach to combat negative thoughts. For example, if we are suffering from stage fright, we need to ask ourselves what kind of thoughts come to our mind at that moment. Catastrophic prediction is common in this case. We tend to think of the worst case scenarios and dwell on the dire consequences. When we become aware of the critical thoughts behind anticipatory fear, we can challenge them. Once it becomes a practice, negative thoughts will stop ruling our lives.

- **Think Rationally and Challenge Negative Thoughts**

Challenge your negative thinking pattern. Whenever you hear a part of you judging yourself, simply say, "Thank you for caring. Tell me what specifically you want me to do? How will this serve me?" Think logically and be prepared for both the good and the bad. Remember the priest who says to a couple getting married, "In life as in death, remain true friends." Approach any result with calmness. It is bound to bring immense happiness.

Though it isn't an easy task, you will be surprised by your own efforts. Maintain a diary. Let the thoughts run. Jot them down. Be reasonable. Don't aim for the sky of happiness and come hurtling down to earth by negative thinking. It is not a Friday box office fortune of a film star that changes one completely overnight.

**Follow these simple points:**

- **Be fair in your thinking.** Try not to be self-centred. It can be very limiting. For instance, next time your spouse complains about your cooking, surprise him by asking, 'Can I make you something else?' Or ask if he would like to order something instead from the restaurant. See the effect!

  Apply this trend of thoughts in other areas of your life too. Your thought energy will help you to enjoy and eventually be happy. And that's exactly what we all are looking for! It's a huge help when a positive thought or action is executed.

- **Things cannot be in your control all the time.** When out of stubbornness or habit, we are unwilling to let go of the issue, more negative thoughts cloud our mind. For a change, choose to be happy than to be right. Let go. Accept the situation and use it to your advantage. If you are stuck in a traffic jam, there is hardly anything you can do about it. Fretting and cursing the system is not going to change the situation. Rather, play feel-good music or a motivational CD or call and catch up with someone you have long been wanting to meet. This will help you change to a more positive state of mind and make the situation more bearable.

- **Stop being paranoid!** This applies to mothers who slog throughout the year to make their children study. They are more paranoid about exams than their wards. Some of them hold themselves responsible for the poor performance of their wards. It could also happen to an athlete who is appearing for the final heats in the Olympic ring. The thought that he might not win makes him feel nervous. Put in your best efforts and leave the rest to God. Success doesn't come overnight. Learn from failures and move ahead. Our positive attitude will ultimately take us to our destination. A small child was auditioned for a school annual play. Just like any other parent, his mother too waited with bated breath for the result fearing how he would react to the disappointment if he was not selected. She smiled to see her son rushing up to her with pride and excitement. "Guess what, mom," he shouted, "I have been chosen to clap and cheer! And my teacher says this is the most important role in the whole act." Hats off to such great teachers who help children see something good in every situation!

> For a change, choose to be happy than to be right.

- **Do not worry about other people's reactions.** We, as performers, generally place expectations on ourselves. Sometimes doubts assail the mind. We fear failure and rejection. Think positive and build up the confidence to tackle the situation. Most celebrities learn to be immune to gossip to remain sane.

Have you ever seen any politician stepping down because some journalist wrote something against him?

Challenge the garbage of your negative thoughts. Shake them off and step up like the farmer's old donkey that fell into a dry well. The farmer tried his best to rescue him but failed. Finally, he decided to bury the donkey in the well itself. He took a spade and started filling the well with debris. The wise donkey shook off the debris as it fell on it and after a while emerged from the well.

## Keep Away From Toxic People

"You are the average of the five people you spend the most time with."

(Jim Rohn, self-made millionaire and successful author)

This means it is important to be in the company of right people. It has been rightly said, "Everyone has the power to make others happy. Some do it by entering the room and some by leaving it." Haven't we all experienced the change in environment and smiles vanishing when even one negative person joins the conversation or enters the room? And the moment he leaves the room, there is happiness all around. There are also those who simply by calling you on the telephone can bring tension, stress, and disorder in your life. Then there are a couple of dream stealers who tell us that our dreams are impossible. They try to dissuade us from believing in ourselves.

Unhappy souls spread gloom and unhappiness everywhere. These people are psychic vampires. They have a limiting effect on our well laid out goals. We better be wary of such people. Keep yourself detached and in control while talking to a negative person as these people know no boundaries. If you succeed in managing your own negative thoughts and behaviour, you have won the battle. Do not get into their trap by getting involved. We all have one or two friends who constantly attempt to bring us down to their level. If so, it's time to move on and make new friends. Choose your friends who are positive and who emit hope. If we are surrounded by happy souls, there is no reason for us to be unhappy. If we have to carry something contagious, why not carry happiness and laughter?

> "Everyone has the power to make others happy. Some do it by entering the room and some by leaving it."

Once there was a race of frogs. The aim was to reach the top of a high tower. Many frogs gathered to see and cheer them. The race started. Most frogs didn't believe that it was possible for anyone to reach the top. All the phrases that one could hear were: "What a pain!!! They will never make it." And the frogs that were in the race began to resign except for one who kept on climbing. The crowd continued, "Impossible!!! He will never make it. No frog has ever achieved such a difficult task." But this one reached the top of the tower. The other frogs wanted to know how he did it. They discovered that the winner frog was deaf. The moral of the story is 'Never listen to negative people because they remove the best aspirations from your heart.'

Make a list of the time you spend regularly with your family members, friends, co-workers, neighbours, and so on. Put a minus sign next to the people who are toxic and a plus sign next to those who are nurturing and positive. Increase the number of positive people in your list and delete those who have a negative influence on you.

Of course, it is ultimately the person's choice whether one is a positive or a negative respondent or thinker. But to free oneself from the negative influences requires a deliberate shift in thinking. Step back and see things from a broader perspective. Investing in our brain is the greatest gain.

"The ego is a terrible taskmaster who drives you to distress. Once your spirit is exhausted, you will be irretrievably lost."

*(The Tao is Tao, 73)*

## Ego – A Friend or a Foe?

A man told his doctor that he wasn't able to do all the things around the house like he used to. The doctor did a complete examination. The eager patient said, "Now, Doc, I can take it. Tell me in plain English what is wrong with me."

"Well, in plain English," the doctor replied, "you've just become lazy."

"Really!" the man looked upset. "But it sounds so middle class. Please do me a favour. Give me the medical term for this condition, so I can tell my family and friends."

Funny, yet true! People have weird ways of feeding their ego. Ego makes one manipulative. It is a tool we use to hide our faults or weaknesses we believe we have. If somebody were to call a six-feet man 'a pygmy' he would just laugh at the ridiculous statement because his height says it all! He doesn't feel the need to prove his point. You pass the same remark to a four-feet guy, he would probably start arguing and justifying! Why? Because, he is insecure! Egoists are quick to take offence.

Egoists live in the make-believe world of being too important and too great. They lose no opportunity to inflate their egos. Most discussions and arguments we observe are an ego massage. "Ha, you should have seen his face when I told him this . . ." boosts one's ego. Often people ask tough questions, to either satisfy their ego by making others uncomfortable, or to cover up their own lack of knowledge, or to impress others. And, not only that! They think that without them the world would have come to an end. Yet, if we could realize that cemetery is full of those people who thought they were indispensable, we would be able to give up our illusions of being superior, better, and great. We need to understand that as human beings, we all share many of the same fears, concerns, hopes, and dreams.

The ego survives and thrives on selfishness. It craves for constant attention and derives sadistic satisfaction from being outright obnoxious at one extreme to being bashful at the other end. When unhindered, the ego adds to the collection of many such disillusioned and judgmental themes, enough to create a sea of unhappiness. As the ego becomes the master, the real self withdraws into a shell. It is full of selfish desire and aversion. When we are in the ego, we are cut off from life with a dark cave full of selfish desires and aversions whose actions and consequences bring only pain and suffering for ourselves and others. Each one of us has some ego problem or the other. The development and the size of the ego depend on our inherited conditioning and life experiences.

We miss the uncomplicated pleasures of life when we covet the luxuries our immediate neighbours have. Keeping up with the material riches of the gilt-edged neighbour can be quite exhausting. The inflated ego creates scaffolding around the mind and isolates the real self. We feed the invisible ego till it traps us.

Consider a camel, the ship of the barren, sandy desert. As the proverb goes, 'A camel prefers the desert to the Himalayas. In the desert he is the Himalaya unto himself!' Meaning that it is the king of all it surveys. The camel knows that no one can cross the desert without it. The ego functions similarly in human beings. It makes one so vulnerable that it becomes a defence mechanism of an individual. It protects the person from stress and other seemingly dangerous situations. The ego creates an army that fortifies the physical and mental well-being almost unconsciously.

> As the ego becomes the master, the real self withdraws into a shell.

It simply means that the ego defends our inherent weaknesses and exploits our ambitions. A hurt ego is capable of shocking its victim. In office, rivalries are mostly a result of ego clashes. Can you imagine how a senior feels when a junior bypasses him and is given a higher post in the organization? The ego of the senior is obviously hurt. He goes into either protective or attack mode, depending on the severity of the situation. A frail ego like this could create unpleasant conditions. The senior could indulge in hurriedly giving his resignation, or, if he is mature, he could handle the change in equations more prudently by having a healthy discussion with the management. But a bloated ego will coerce him to fight for survival and avoid further humiliation. If the ego intervenes, it is likely to leave a permanent emotional scar. Many bosses are more concerned with their own ego satisfaction rather than the interest of the company. Due to their ego, these people start giving themselves extra cover of false perceptions. The fragile ego makes them completely dependent on what others think of them.

Ego problems are not restrained only up to offices or societies, but are very much present inside our homes. It can be seen between all the relations—father-son, husband-wife, brother-

brother, or brother-sister. No relationship is left untouched by the ego problem. Nowadays, young school-going boys or girls also have huge egos to satisfy. This is a common problem in any peer group from five years to seventy years! With the advent of new technologies and advancement in higher education, the problem is worsening. Sometimes others' opinions become so important that a person forgets the valued opinions of his own family. A youngster may want to spend nights away in the discos and hang out with friends against his parent's wishes. Result? An ego fracas is waiting to explode like a time bomb. If you are finding others' opinions more important than your own or those of your family, it is time to demarcate your priorities.

The ego makes us live in a make-believe world where we feel something is lacking or has gone astray. It dwells in the past or the future but never lives for the present, which is far more important. The problem is that we lack the will to be happy with what we have. We hanker so much after what we don't but others have, that simple pleasures elude us. One of our neighbours has a very beautiful bungalow. She was very happy and proud until lately, when one of her friends built a mansion right next to her house. Her ego could not digest it. She went into serious depression for days together. How can one be happy when the grass looks greener at the other end!

> When we operate from the higher self, we are open to healthy discussions rather than arguments.

## Cracking the Subtle Ego

To salvage our happiness, we need to let the ego out of hiding. Yet, it isn't easy to wipe out the traces of the ego. This is not water off a duck's back. But it can be accomplished by a wide variety of techniques.

## Operate from higher self

All humans function either from lower self or higher self. Our environment and our responses to the environment determine which self is more dominant in us—higher or lower.

I don't know how many of us are aware that when we are born we have an inherent cosmic intelligence. There are other descriptions of this knowledge—intuition, ESP (extra sensory perceptions), developed inner voice, etc. But as we grow, we are bombarded with knowledge of the outside world, which is like adding more bricks to the wall. It only leads to sheltering more mind viruses. We are programmed to behave in a certain way. In other words, we acquire knowledge from different sources and our perceptions undergo changes which in turn change our behaviour and the way we perceive certain situations.

Ideally, we should function with both the knowledge—acquired and the inherent. For instance, when we deal with a certain situation, experience teaches us how to behave and present ourselves to others. But sometimes, the situation may warrant using more than just acquired knowledge. This is where higher knowledge comes in use. This is when heroes are born. In April 2007, a video tape was released—a perfect example of operating from higher self. One of the lions manages to catch a young buffalo calf from a herd of buffalo. But the herd fights back for the life of the calf and eventually chases the lion off—thus changing the rules of the jungle. Unfortunately, the gift that we are born with is left unexplored. It remains embedded in the subconscious mind. It is seen and experienced only in emergencies. That is the time people respond more to their inner selves than the rules of survival. We need to bring awareness to this fact in our life and do something about it to bring out the 'real us' in us. Awareness allows space for improvement which leads to development of the true self. It removes unwanted emotions. This means the situation becomes an opportunity to grow inward—(move higher) rather than get threatened by the situation and become rigid in responses.

The ego belongs to lower self. When we use the lower self, it affects every relationship. The ego wants to prove it is right, always. When we operate from the higher self, we are open to healthy discussions rather than arguments. A person who does not have an ego, automatically gains respect. Speaking the truth gives us satisfaction and happiness. When we speak the truth, we are in a relationship that is interdependent. It is on us—what we want to live with—a higher self that we were born with or the lower self that has been acquired over the years. It simply means, either we let the ego (lower self) enslave us or be the masters of our ego by operating from our higher self.

## Still on that silly ego trip?

A stubborn ego may not accept the change so easily. A boastful ego defends itself even if it is wrong as it happened with Mulla Nasiruddin.

Mulla Nasiruddin made life impossible for his associates because he believed he was infallible. Finally one of them spoke up. "Nasiruddin," he said, "You surely have not been right all the time?"

"There was one time I was wrong," admitted the Mulla. "When was that?" asked the surprised worker. He could not believe that Nasiruddin would ever admit that he was ever wrong, even once. He could not believe his own ears. "The one time," recalled Mulla Nasiruddin, "when I thought I was wrong, but I was really not."

With an ego like that can one ever become happy? Misplaced pride (many communities have that in India), determined ego (rigid rules, traditions, rituals), and ambitions lead to misery, not happiness.

The road to happiness is straight. Loosen your mental hinges and welcome the changes. Just as you require regular exercise to keep the body fit, you need to enjoy the simple pleasures of life by shunting the ego at the back of the beyond. As you do it regularly, you will find the ego melting. Do not become the shadow of your ego. Shel Silverstein has described this in a poem:

The Shadow Race
Every time I've raced my shadow
When the Sun was at my back,
It always ran ahead of me
Always got the best of me.
But every time I have chased my shadow
When my face was towards the Sun,
I won.

Cemetery is full of those people who thought they were indispensable.

## Go that extra mile:

Here are some simple techniques to shed your ego. For your good, get armed:

- Are you always looking for appreciation—on your looks, clothes, material riches, grades or salary or even dropping big names? Are you moving in powerful circles and then flaunt your big contacts amongst common people and friends? It is time to make a change. There is fear of your falling prey to the ego. The ego loves praise. Humbly accept compliments but don't go hunting for them.

- Do those bold outfits make you vulnerable to strange looks or appraisals? There is a danger of the ego going overboard. Try not to attract too much attention. Stop talking loudly, if you do. Replace sarcasm with silence or if you cannot keep quiet, say something sober. Stop cracking jokes at someone else's expense. Here, ego is at play.

- Do you have superiority complex? Do you feel you are more intelligent than the others in your group? Be sure, the ego is rearing its ugly head. It can hamper your growth. Change your attitude and change the group, if need be. Being in the company of people better than us, gives us more scope to learn and grow.

- Are you really happy in the company of those who flatter you constantly, whereas inside you know that they are not true? Try to be truthful, first to your own self and then to others. The company that you keep should motivate you towards higher self and not make you an egoist. If you have a coterie, do away with it. Make genuine friends.

- There is no such thing as healthy gossip. Walk away from gossip if it is demeaning. Protest, if need be. Don't keep silent and stay on it, as that would mean you are agreeing. The ego will try to take sides. But you need to ask yourself what is right.

- The ego bobs up in everyday situations. Hurt egos look for revenge. Don't get carried away when the responses are contrary. Being aware will keep you composed and you will realize your true identity.

Stop feeding your ego. Take it down a few notches. Be delighted to see your happiness curve going up!

"Men are not prisoners of fate,
but only prisoners of their own minds."
(Franklin D. Roosevelt, Pan American Day address,
April 15, 1939)

# The Noisy Mind

An elephant was standing and picking leaves from a tree. A small fly came buzzing near his ear. The elephant waved it away with his long ears. The fly came again, and the elephant waved it away once more.

This was repeated several times. Then the elephant asked the fly: "Why are you so restless and noisy? Why can't you stay for a while in one place?"

The fly answered: "I am attracted to whatever I see, hear, or smell. My five senses pull me constantly in all directions and I cannot resist them. What is your secret? How can you stay so calm and still?"

The elephant stopped eating and said:

"My five senses do not rule my attention. Whatever I do, I get immersed in it. Now that I am eating, I am completely immersed in eating. In this way, I can enjoy my food and chew it better. I rule and control my attention, and not the other way around."

The Katha Upanishad (1.3.3-4) compares the body to a chariot—the senses are like horses, the mind is like the reins (driving force), and the intelligence is like the driver. The soul is the passenger within the chariot. The senses are powerful and capable of moving us in any direction. Though the mind is more powerful than the senses, it is the senses that govern our lives. Most people waste their time in gratifying their senses. Out of the thousands and even millions of ignorant people, just one reaches the platform of knowledge and understands higher values of life. Such a person is a *jnani*. He knows all actions will bind him to material existence and cause transmigration from one kind of body to another. A jnani is considered superior to a *karmi* because he does not blindly follow his senses.

Our mind is the most valuable possession we have. It is just that we don't treat it like one. We fail to control our thoughts and let all sorts of meaningless thoughts enter and occupy space in our mind. According to scientists, nearly fifty thousand thoughts flit in and out of our minds daily. And how many of these are useful? Probably very few, as most thoughts are related to worry, anger, jealousy, future, or the past. The way viruses weaken the immune system physically, unwarranted thoughts rot the mind from inside. And in their rottenness, these unhappy souls spread more unhappiness around. The most powerful tool that has the power to bring for us heaven on earth has become a source of our miseries.

It is our thoughts that shape our experiences and design our lives. Bad thoughts drain us out of the energy. Good thoughts produce positive energy. Our life is a reflection of our thoughts—chosen consciously or unconsciously. To change our lives we need to change our experiences and to change our experiences we need to think differently and work on our thoughts.

No wonder, down the years, philosophers, guides, and intellectuals have future generations pondering with:

- Master your thoughts and you master your mind.

- Master your mind and you master your life.

- Master your life and you master your destiny.

An obedient and disciplined mind always finds happiness.

## Taming the Mind

> "It's not enough to have a good mind;
> the main thing is to use it well."
>
> (Rene Descartes)

Gautam Buddha in circa 500 BC summed up his Awakening (also referred as Enlightenment) by saying, "There is nothing as disobedient as an undisciplined mind, and there is nothing obedient as a disciplined mind." He said that the mind is like a bird. If you tighten the leash, it suffocates and if the leash is loose, it slips.

The mind is really like a pachyderm. When tamed it is a gentle giant. Let loose or leave it untrained, it can ruin a manicured garden in minutes. Proper discretion and judgment is necessary to tame it. Remember that no one can tame and discipline our mind for us except us and only us.

Let's take the first step towards understanding the mind.

> The way viruses weaken the immune system physically, unwarranted thoughts rot the mind from inside.

## Recognize the vagaries of the mind

The mind is in constant motion. It thinks even while we are asleep. So during the waking state we can imagine what happens. Some people are so caught up with their thoughts that they are seen talking to themselves. People around them feel they are insane. But the truth is that most normal people talk to themselves endlessly all day—quietly in their heads.

We can compare our mind to a radio where we have a number of sounds and stations available for us. It is our choice, which one to listen to. However, sometimes we get so addicted to a particular station that we forget about the better options available. The tuner gets rusted. Similarly, when we get addicted to some particular negative thoughts, they become our reality. Habitual thinkers tend to worry and create a mess of their lives.

Whenever a thought enters the mind, it elicits the senses to act or react. During one of the cricket matches between India and Pakistan, it became quite evident that India would lose. Reactions of some fans were varied: some were violent and threw bottles on the ground. Some fans collapsed and fainted. One felt the sense of loss so strongly that he died of a heart attack watching it on television! The Indian captain said very calmly in a press conference after the loss, "After all it is only a game!" But fans took it too seriously. Each fan knew it was a game, but for some, it was a matter of life and death. The addiction to the game and the resultant madness and chaos was a deadly combination which allowed minds to go haywire. This happens when we let our minds lose.

If one is in control of the mind and can comprehend its nature, it would be so much easier to be happy. If we can control the thought process, we can control the mind. By changing our thought process and values, we can get the mind under our leash.

## Be resilient to change

As we grow older, we all get out of the 'my dad strongest!' syndrome. We realize that our dad is not a superman. We get to know that our favourite heroes too have 'feet of clay.' Understanding and accepting change in the right spirit and at the right time can do wonders to our health (both physical and mental) and happiness. When the rock that embeds the diamond is scraped off, the sparkle and shine of the latter becomes visible. The mind, in the same way, is embedded in defilement, craving, clinging, and complete darkness. When our cutting tools—mindfulness and discernment—filter it out, the internal structure of the mind shows its own accord.

It is not a difficult task if we set our mind to it. So often we have heard, "I achieved this (a goal) because I set my mind to it." Ask any beauty pageant queen. She will say, "I watched the former winners and decided that when I grow up I shall win the crown for myself and my country." Mind you, this is said when she is very much in her pre-teens. So after many years of visualizing, grooming, and participating, one day she becomes Miss Universe or Miss World. She consciously applies her mind to her goal with a single-minded determination. If we seriously study this example we will realize the girl's happiness was her goal. Then why, after winning, does she rejoice for a year or so and then goes into oblivion? That is because her goal was short lived. She did not apply her mind to what will happen after that. When the reality dawns on her it is kind of too late. She struggles like everyone else. If at this stage, she once again applies her mind and determines to make the paradigm shift, she can still achieve happiness and make others happy around her too.

Do you get angry or use cuss words and spoil the entire day because of the unnecessary honking when stuck in the traffic jam? Do you brood all day long when you are wronged by your dear ones? We generally tend to fill our minds with such trivial thoughts. This happens when we fail to use our senses sensibly—the eyes are used to watch television endlessly, the ears used to hear unnecessary gossip, and the brain used to read mindless literature. We might believe that as human beings it is natural to get affected by situations. But if we give a thought to every trivial thing or person we come across in our lives, when will we have time or the energy for things more important? It is most likely that we will become an average, reactionary person without the capacity to create our own world. Eventually, the price paid is quite heavy. Make right use of your senses and streamline your thoughts in the right direction. Be positive and be aware of your capabilities and limitations. Apply the price and the pay-off technique to train your mind and change your values. Put on the blinkers if you have to accomplish specific goals.

If we can discipline the erring thoughts, we can lead a much better life.

## Transform the mental state

It is easier to control the mind only if one surrenders completely and becomes aware. Lord Krishna professed and extolled this message in the celestial song Bhagwat Gita, millions of years ago.

Here is an example of doing things with awareness and with little or no awareness. The first time when I was learning to drive, I was fully focused on what I did and every movement I made. I used to be fully present in the present. Gradually as I started to gain mastery, the task became automatic. I could drive, talk on the mobile, and listen to the music, all at the same time. My mind multitasked, and I could drive without being aware.

All our problems come from lack of awareness. The most effective tool that can help us to fight the devil is 'awareness.' Bring awareness in whatever you think. Be alert. We don't have to change the thoughts. The simple act of noticing our thoughts frees us of them. It has a magical quality which in the course of life gets paralyzed or channelled into one-sidedness by mind viruses. Be a witness to every act of yours—the way you walk, talk, eat, breathe, everything. Make the mind focus on the present state. It will come with regular practice. If you are eating, think of what you are chewing. If you are walking, think of the steps you take. When you focus on the present, the mind will wander less. Increasing watchfulness will provide the clarity of mind. It will reduce the internal chattering and bring your true potential to the surface.

> If we give a thought to every trivial thing or person we come across in our lives, when will we have time or the energy for things more important?

Once we are aware of our thoughts, we will be amazed at the inordinate amount of time spent on intangible things like brooding over the past or worrying over a possible future. It will bring the chaos to order. Now that you know that the seed of a positive or negative mind is the responsibility of thoughts, make a mantra to alleviate the thought process. There is no point in coping up with zillions of thoughts in a directionless mind. Use the higher force to empower the mind. Remember the schooldays? When the higher force (principal) was on the rounds, everything used to be in order. When the principal was on leave, there was total disorder. Bring the school discipline back to life. Focus the mind on more productive goals. Life is too short to be fettered away in mindless games and errant activity.

Follow these simple steps:

- Listen to the voice of the mind. Use intelligence and discern what is right and what is wrong. If a particular thought pattern is returning, it is time to take stock of what is wrong. When you are being alert to it, you are aware of its consequences.

- Every night, empty your mind. Don't think of the day's events—good or bad. When you remove the garbage of thoughts, you allow new thoughts to be processed.

- Meditate. The state of stillness will make you peaceful and happy.

## Learn to remain silent

If speech is silver, we all know silence is golden. The stillness of the nature and the universe teaches us to become rock steady. Silence communicates in many ways. Just being together sometimes in silence calms the troubled mind. Have you observed sometimes, two old people sitting quietly and happily on a bench? These are times when words are profane. Yet some people get uncomfortable with silence. They try to strike a conversation even when there is nothing to say. If others feel you are dumb when silent, so be it. Let them take their time to understand the power of keeping quiet.

> We don't have to change the thoughts. The simple act of noticing our thoughts frees us of them.

Silence is to be experienced and not understood. Unyoke the mental hinges and experience the silence. Silence speaks volumes, when understood on a higher level. In ancient times *rishis* and *munis* kept '*maun vrat*' (silence) as a part of their meditative techniques. Bring yourself to that level.

Remember, when words come out of the mouth, they are only the final arrows. The thoughts have already been formed in the mind. Therefore, 'think before you speak.' Let the mind be pure in all its thoughts, words, and deeds. Reach the stage when you can smile at the voice in your head.

"Burn the candles, use nice bed sheets, wear the fancy lingerie.
Don't save it for special occasions. Today is special."

(Regina Brett)

## Living in the Past

"*The last time I hugged someone was when my friend left for college in August. Even then, it was just a quick embrace that friends give each other. Hugging makes me feel so uncomfortable. My mom and dad used to hug me, but I always pulled away, so they haven't tried in a long time.*

*I know I sound silly, but I don't like being touched. My friends ask 'Why?' But I shrug. I can't tell them the truth. I can't tell them that when I was eleven, I was raped, and from that moment I haven't been able to accept affection from people.*

*Believe me, I want it so bad that I cry. In fact, I'm crying right now, but I just don't know how to let people hold me like that. Especially the ones I love. It was nine years ago that it happened, but it's still fresh in my mind, in my dreams.*"

Though it took a couple of years for this girl to seek professional help to get rid of her painful past memories, at last she is able to live a normal life. But there are some who are so used to living in the past that they never get to taste the pleasures of the present.

## Are you wedded to the past?

Sometimes things happen in our lives that are very painful. A parent may have been abusive, a partner unfaithful, a good friend may have betrayed us in some way. These are life-shattering experiences. Then there are things that happen in our day-to-day lives—experiences that are not quite as devastating, but painful enough to screw up our happiness. For example, our project is rejected, our spouse says something nasty to us in anger, our colleague is getting married and we are not in the list of invitees. Generally, we find it quite difficult to recover from such experiences. Some of us never do, completely. We blame the situations. Whereas, in reality, it is not the situation, but our reaction to the situation which is responsible for our long-lasting painful experiences. When thoughts circle around our history (past experiences) they create hopes or fears. Bad experiences create fear and worry. Pleasant experiences give hope. Unfortunately, we humans tend to recall negative memories more than the positive ones—thus, never allowing ourselves to enjoy the bliss of the present.

Possessions add clutter, so do past memories. Past memories become shadows and refuse to leave us, which further add to our stressful lives. The obsession with the past becomes paranoia. We become resentful, angry, sad, remorseful, jealous, and unforgiving. We slowly develop a negative attitude. Negative thinking happens with constant attachment to the past failures. All the bitterness becomes a part of our character. We lose self-control and ruin important relationships.

We all get habituated to clinging to the past because of its comfort level. We do not like to be shaken out of the comfort zone. With the result, the past memories keep haunting us, never allowing us to live in the present. They bite like a pebble in the shoe and make us limp, denying any happiness or satisfaction along the way. However pleasant the surroundings may be, these pebbles never allow us to enjoy life. We are left frustrated and plagued with the pain. We keep carrying the baggage, till it weighs us down.

Our lives are shaped not only by significant events of our past but also by events which we anticipate eagerly. Some people ruin their happiness quotient by being too apprehensive about the future. They are so engrossed with building up a bright future that it takes away all the joy and happiness of their present moment. We had an officer who always deprived himself and his family of small pleasures of life which he could very well afford. His logic was that he was saving it all for a wonderful life after retirement. On the last day of his retirement, he had a sudden heart attack and passed away within seconds. God bless his soul! It left me wondering, do we really have to plan and wait for so long to live a happy life! Why can't we work towards our goals and enjoy the present moment at the same time? There are people who look forward to a 'holiday,' but when the time comes, they are worried about completing their annual marketing plan in the office. How will such a person enjoy the sights and sounds of the holiday? Even if we are preparing for the future, we need to be aware of the 'NOW' so that we do not miss out noticing what's happening in the present, where the building blocks for the future are being set up.

> Possessions add clutter,
> so do past memories.

Unwarranted past memories need to be discarded with the passage of time. Make peace with the past so it won't screw up your present. Do not waste your precious energy on issues of the past, negative thoughts, or things you cannot control. Instead, invest your energy in the positive present moment.

If while reading this book, your thoughts are on how rude one of your colleagues was to you or what is to be done for tomorrow's meeting or deciding the lunch menu for a party two days later, you are living simultaneously in the past and the future. This is one of the reasons for your living a not-so-happy life.

## Magic of being in the present

Very often, when we are caught in life-and-death situations, they bring out the best in us. The soldier on the battlefield at an altitude of thirty thousand feet knows he is in a do-or-die situation fighting for his country. He lives and dies for that moment. Heroes are those who live in the present. These are the times when you cannot think of past or future. There is no time to fear, have grudges, or become paranoid. These are magical moments. You have to be alert, aware, and present in 'the now' to react to the events happening.

Let me narrate one such magical moment of my life.

One fine day in Pune Cantt, the weather was just perfect for reading a novel in the sun along with a hot cup of tea. I was doing just that when slowly I fell asleep. In my dream, I dreamt that an ugly black snake was moving near my leg and trying to climb up my body. I opened my eyes and realized to my utter horror that it was not a dream but a truly horrendous snake creeping up on me. I don't know how and when I caught him by the tail and threw him away. It's a different story as to how the snake was killed by the orderlies and how I passed out afterwards.

"How did this happen?" I wondered. The answer was simple and led to a great awakening. There was no time to fear. It was pure action. There was no thinking about the past or the future. What mattered was the present moment.

The magic of the present is like the thrill of surfing or hunting. We need not necessarily indulge in such dangerous sports to get the thrill. We can experience the same every day and every moment by being in the present. At the same time we can enjoy living life to the fullest.

## De-clutter the past

Losers live in the past, beggars live in the future. Blissful moments are here and now. Those who live in these moments, live life king size. Whether you want to live the life of a loser, beggar, or an emperor; a blissful life or miserable one—it's for you to decide.

Well, to bring in the power of 'NOW' in your life is a form of art that can be mastered.

## Live for the simple pleasures of life

I have noticed over a period of time that in parties and social gatherings certain people are generally not enjoying the party. Mentally, they are thousands of miles away as if waiting for something—to win a lottery or a contest, get a better job or a vacation, and be the richest man or a successful businessman. All their activities are future-oriented, focussed only on becoming and achieving something. Waiting is a state of the mind. It means you don't want the present, but the future. One of my friends always wished to have a one-karat diamond ring. But the day her husband bought her one, she started dreaming of a two-karat ring. The problem does not lie in setting higher goals, but the problem starts when these goals become everything and engulf our present moments of happiness.

Are you also waiting for the tall dark and handsome man to sweep you off your feet? Are you looking for a friend who understands you? Are you looking for the perfect mate for your pet? Do you live to get the next model of the cellular phone or car? No wonder life is depressing! Chances are that happiness will be around, not with you. You become the creator of your own misery. One day you will run out of steam and wonder what the hell were you chasing! By wise reflection, we can understand how these beliefs create misery in our lives. Small pleasures of life are the little everyday happenings—the lovely Chinese dinner, the cocktail at the bar, eating popcorns and watching a movie, etc.

If you are not feeling happy at this moment, become aware of what you are doing at present. Ask yourself: "Is there any enjoyment in what I am doing, or is there a feeling of burden?" If you are not satisfied, it means the past or the future is covering up your present moments. You seem to be focussing more on the results. You need not change 'what' you are doing. You need to change the 'how.'

As soon as we honour the present moment, all unhappiness and struggle is dissolved and life begins to flow with joy and ease. Our happiness no more depends on others. Since we already feel happy and contented on a deeper level, there is a playful, joyous energy behind whatever we do, which in turn produces better results.

> Losers live in the past, beggars live in the future. Blissful moments are here and now.

## Live from the centre

There are two ways to live life. One is to live from the boundary and the other is to live from the centre. From the boundary, there is reaction, not action. In a way, we are just a slave of the circumstances. When we live from our centre, we are in the acting mode which in turn produces more positive results. For instance, how do you feel when you are abused? If you are centred, you will be indifferent to the abuse. If you are on the periphery, you will get angry and react. Same way if we love from the periphery, it will not be total. The rest of the space will be filled with jealousy, hatred, or expectations. But if we love from the centre, it is total. There is no space for toxic thoughts such as anger or misunderstandings.

Most of us act from centre only in life-and-death situations, where we cannot think beyond saving ourselves or how scary it's going to be, as it happened with me in Pune. Sometime back there was an interesting news on one of the news channels. A handicapped man got caught in the flood. It was extremely difficult for him to keep his feet grounded in the turbulent water, but he somehow managed to stand in the water for twenty-four hours and survived. How did he do that? Simple! He stayed centered.

## Bring awareness in whatever you do

We can live life in two ways:

First, enjoy the temporary gratifications such as sex, indulging in food, accumulating things, sleeping for long hours, living in inertia or aggression, and second, move towards awareness. But then there is no difference between animals and us. A bear sleeps for hours together; animals enjoy as much sexual pleasure as human beings; bees and ants collect food as human beings collect money, property, things, wealth, throughout life. What differentiates human beings from animals is the choice of going upward or downward. When we cling on to something or somebody and are constantly struggling, resisting, controlling, and manipulating, we are going downward. We end up feeling frustrated, frightened, and depressed. When we enjoy life without getting attached to it, we are moving upward which is the prerogative of human beings.

Enjoy when it's there, let go when it's gone. When we let go, we no longer expect conditions for them to be anything other than what they are.

Being continuously aware is the technique for centring—for achieving the inner fire. We might fail once or twice, but will succeed, ultimately. Bringing awareness to our obsessions and addictions— their source and fear of change makes it easy for us to bring in the required changes. Once a drunkard realizes he is drinking too much, he automatically is on the path of becoming sober.

Happiness does not come with years. It comes with moments. Remember the value of each moment. Somebody rightly said that time is like a river. You cannot touch the same water twice, because the flow that has passed will never pass again. Love and treat each moment like a precious diamond.

If we are truly aware, we will know that no one can promise us anything. From moment to moment, there are so many changes—in situations, emotions, and the body chemistry. All we can do is to be open and receptive to the moment itself and say to ourselves, "This is the moment!" To depend on a promise is to invite sadness, for though it may be given in good faith, it may lose its validity with the changes which occur in time. This main awareness must permeate all parts of our consciousness. What we need to do is, make an 'attempt' to live in the present moment—a positive start in the right direction.

## In brief:

**First**, be conscious of what you think. Make a mental note whenever you find yourself focussing on something negative. Most likely, your negative feelings are based on something from your past, or something you fear in your future.

**Second**, write down on a piece of paper, some of the negative thoughts that come up more than others. If in a few days, you find this exercise helpful, then by all means, go back and work on a few more issues. Just take it easy. No rush, no pressure.

**Third**, look at these negative thoughts for a minute. The ones that are from your past, even if it was just yesterday, put a 'P' next to them. The ones that are worries or fears of something in your future, even if it is tomorrow, mark with an 'F.'

**Fourth**, take some time to 'brainstorm' with these thoughts. Are they things that are totally out of your control? Or something from your past, that there is no way to change? Cancel these thoughts. Take some time to jot down different ideas of how you might reconcile with the issues still remaining. There is no right or wrong way to do this. Do it in whatever way you want.

> To depend on a promise is to invite sadness, for though it may be given in good faith, it may lose its validity with the changes which occur with time.

This process is about awareness—nothing more, nothing less. We need to be 'aware' of our thoughts, not let them run wildly in our head. This is the first and the most important step to live in the present moment. Even if we are in the moment just for a few minutes a day, it is worth it.

So when these thoughts come into your head, remind yourself that once again your past is getting ready to have a ball at your expense. Ask yourself if you are aware of that. The question itself will bring you back in the present. Just be at peace with the present moment, and with yourself. Life is a roller coaster and the sooner we understand it, the better. Enjoy the ride to its fullest. Be happy! Because if not now, then when?

"There is a great deal of pain in life and perhaps the
only pain that can be avoided is the pain
that comes from trying to avoid pain."

(R. D. Laing)

## Suppressed Pain

Raghav, a fifty-five-year-old man in Mumbai joined an EFT (Emotional Freedom Technique) workshop. All the people present were asked the reasons for joining this workshop. Some wanted to learn public speaking skills, some wanted to get over fear, and some wanted to get over phobia of noises. This man astounded all by saying he wanted to forget the pain his father had inflicted upon him as a child. Whenever he remembered his father hitting his mother or banging her head against the walls for some frivolous reason, he used to get enraged. He wanted to kill his father as a nine-year-old and he nurtured those feelings even at this age. But fear, anger, and future anxiety stopped him. All these years he buried the monumental pain in his heart. He tried hard to get rid of the frustration and helplessness of his childhood, but in vain. With the result, it had started affecting his normal life. He lacked the courage to ask for a raise even after many years of work. He was scared and confused. He could not fulfil his family obligations due to fear of failure. He chose to join the workshop to feel 'normal.'

If past has such a powerful influence on our lives, imagine the case of some phobic who carries an emotional baggage of pain for a lifetime. We may or may not remember a happy occasion, but any event that has caused hurt and pain stays in our mind. We keep on thinking about things which bring unhappiness. Since we do not allow ourselves to let go of those unpleasant feelings, they become our present as was the case with the old man. These painful feelings manifest physically and psychologically and end up killing the very core of rationality.

> Suppressed feelings always look for some outlet. If we don't let them out, they let themselves out through some organ via some illness.

## The mechanism of pain

Reflect on these fundamental lines depicting the cycle of pain:

Pain in the present is experienced as hurt.

Pain in the past is remembered as anger.

Pain in the future is perceived as anxiety.

Guilt is an unexpressed anger redirected against oneself.

Depression is the depletion of energy that occurs when anger is redirected inwards.

The cycle tells that pain is responsible for a wide range of psychological problems or distress which eventually reflects on one's happiness quotient. Pain itself arises out of various emotional states. At the same time, it results in responses that may strengthen and lengthen the pain till it becomes an itch. The more we scratch, the more it itches till it becomes a deep wound. This process becomes an integral part of our lives. We keep falling for it again and again. So much so that we start getting a kind of pleasure, burning in the agony of suppressed pain. Our whole life goes waste in scratching the itch.

So often one hears, "Don't talk about the past. It is painful." Yeah, sure it is. But then it is unhealthy too. Storing such emotions is dangerous. Concealed pain gets embedded in our psyche. Eckhart Tolle, a successful author calls the suppressed pains as pain body. The negative energy is created by emotions stored in the body when they do not find an outlet. Pain of the past, the present, and the future makes our lives go haywire. The dormant pain re-awakens at odd times taking us by surprise. The self-control goes in a tizzy. It robs us of our dignity leaving us embarrassed and ashamed. Sometimes it costs us our job, sometimes a relationship, and sometimes peace of mind. Such is the devastating effect of unsorted emotions.

## What You Resist Persists

We all like the 'happy' emotions. But not many people like dealing with the darker ones—fear, anxiety, disappointment, shame . . . Because we don't like them generally, we deny them. Different people do it in different ways. Some resort to alcohol, some turn to drugs, some blow it in smoke, and some behind a forced smile. You must have watched a friend smiling with misty eyes and insisting, "I'm ok, really." We wait till we explode. No astrologer can predict that day of disastrous explosion.

If you are not aware of the effects of holding back excess emotional baggage, here is for you to know what it can do to you in the long run. Just as a computer stores away junk and obsolete files, so does our mind and body. When emotions are held back, they turn into chronic body scars. The more you suppress, the more painful it gets. It is well known that suppressed feelings always look for some outlet. If we don't let these feelings out, the suppressed feelings can harm our health by effecting our internal organs or by causing some serious illness to our body. Emotional energy gets clogged in arteries, stomach, colon, throat, or chest. Emotional stuffiness is the root cause of coughs, colds, chest pain, or asthma. Sometimes, it results in chronic diseases like cancer, diabetes, or even TB. Moreover suppression leads to blocking of creativity. A hollow chest, a hunchback, reflects a life of grief and burden. Jeff Levin says, "The issue is in the tissue." Caroline Myrs elaborates, "Your biography becomes your biology."

Provoking can rekindle the past trauma unexpectedly and sometimes violently too. Years of suppression are bound to create a revolution. France, Europe, India, African-Asians in America revolted against the apartheid, racial, and cultural abuse. They revolted collectively. It happens at an individual level too. A lone ranger is capable of becoming a jackal when riled. No wonder psychosomatic diseases need cure at the mind level.

Time can heal physical wounds not mental. It would be better to talk over and get over. But how many have the ability to confront the demons within? Not everyone is wise enough like Raghav. Some of us carry it all to our graves.

There is only one way to get to the other side of feelings—feel, deal, and heal. The sooner we realize, the better it is.

## Supermen do cry

'Tough guys don't dance.' 'Men don't cry.' There could be nothing more illogical than these words. There's an old song called, "Don't Cry Out Loud. Just keep it inside. Learn how to hide your feelings." It's simply ridiculous! A man is an emotional creature. If he can get angry, hurt, disillusioned, or emotional, how is it possible for him to not feel pain or cry? Children are so comfortable at emoting. Watch a child tripping. The moment he finds a member of his family around, he starts crying to draw attention. In some instances he does not think twice before bursting out in anger with "You are bad." Or even "I hate you." And within a few seconds, he acts as if nothing has happened. When a young man wants to shed tears over a broken love affair he is branded as a 'sissy.' He is forced to behave in a certain way. Why?

Where does the problem lie? The problem lies in our social upbringing. We normally suppress our feelings due to social constraints. 'Big boys don't cry' has been fed in our minds. In effect, we lose our natural ability to emote because our parents, teachers, and society train us to suppress, not express. In our adult life we have perfected the art of restraint, but in the process have become a sad joker of circumstances. It becomes our second nature. We are finally considered an adult when we are adept at suppressing our natural exuberance that is found unacceptable by society. But habitual suppression of feelings leads to more complications. We become walking time bombs, ready to explode.

> Become conscious when you are reacting to the suppressed pain. Initially, it may be just an irritant, a flash of anger, or some physical symptoms.

The changing equations in society today have altered these 'manly' perceptions to some extent. The metro-sexual male (whatever that means) today does not feel ashamed to shed a tear. Tenderness is slowly beginning to make its effect. How many have admired the Raymond's commercial featuring a man in a suit looking after his pet dogs or introducing his new wife to old school chums? Viewers are now questioning cinema and television soap operas that have survived on revenge themes and anger-driven protagonists. Some people are becoming bold and releasing their negative emotions. It is a good sign. Otherwise how do we account for new hobbies, clubs introducing novel themes, workshops and seminars to deal with stress and anger management? A lot more has to change. Age-old society norms need to be discarded in favour of inner growth.

# Dealing with the welcome itch!

Do you hate someone so much that you would rejoice at his loss? Would you be compelled to avenge your father who never let you become a singer but forced you to become an engineer? Today you have an alternative. Become an engineer-singer. Release the untapped negative emotions creatively. This is one harmless way of handling pain effectively. Now that you have become an engineer, dad cannot stop you from singing. Can he? If he still can, then the problem lies with you.

I don't say that feelings that cause the pain are never justified. Yet, it is in our own interest to release the negative feelings rather than suppressing them, and express inappropriate behaviour at inappropriate times. Nobel Laureate poet Rabindranath Tagore was at his creative best at the time of intense grief. His poetry continued to be his release even after he lost his wife, son, and daughter. Tagore pleads to the Almighty in his book *Gitanjali:*

"When the heart is hard and parched up, come upon
me with a shower of mercy.
When grace is lost from life, come with a burst of song.
When tumultuous work raises its din on all sides shutting me
from beyond, come to me, my lord of silence,
with thy past and rest.
When my beggarly heart sits crouched, shut up in a corner,
break open the door, my king, and come with
the ceremony of a king.
When desire blinds the mind with delusion and dust,
O thou holy one, thou wakeful, come with
light and thy thunder."

Use your suppressed pain as an opportunity to enlighten yourself. Helen Keller says in *We Bereaved* (1929), "When one door of happiness closes, another opens; but often we look so long at the closed door that we do not see the one which has been opened for us."

We all have the natural ability to release ourselves from the pain and get out of the vicious cycle of emotions, if only we make a conscious effort.

## Bring consciousness to your suppressed pain and observe

The best way out of emotional pain is through it. St. Paul said,

"Everything is shown up by being exposed to the light, and whatever is exposed to the light itself becomes light."

When we are aware of the emotions, we can keep a track of the thoughts and feelings. If we start observing, instead of ignoring or pacifying them, we have taken the first step towards dealing with the demon. When we know the cause, we can take the next step.

Become conscious when you are reacting to the suppressed pain. Initially, it may be just an irritant, a flash of anger or some physical symptoms. Whatever it is, catch it before it takes over your thought processes. Here I remember the pearls of wisdom from my father: 'Never promise anything when you are in joy; never open your mouth when you are angry or in pain.' Remain alert. Give it your full attention. Watch the turbulence going on inside you. Accept it. Catch it every time it recurs. Examine what makes you feel pained and depressed. Jot it down rather than allowing any negative thought to make you react adversely. This will enable you to think of creative ways to flush it out of your system. Understand your senses and slowly you will find yourself making peace with your mind. Once the realization dawns, we can stop hurting others and ourselves. We are then at the highest stage of understanding our real selves. Our spontaneous action is no longer negative. The understanding is based on our free selves, without the hindrance of the negative energy.

Enjoy the game. See yourself smiling. Soon you will be able to tackle it with more ease and rationality.

## Listen to your body clock

Executives today have more or less the same schedule. They work crazily from Mondays to Fridays, drown their sorrows in spirits on weekends, crash out on Sundays, and get back to the dirge on Monday mornings. Naturally, anyone will have Monday morning blues with this sort of lifestyle. But how many people have the guts to change this pattern? Sometimes pain becomes the comfort zone. Illness is hidden or forgotten, but never cured. Even a visit to the clinic is seen as a source of embarrassment or a waste of time, unless it is an emergency. Trudging that extra mile to happiness is seen as a huge hurdle.

So how do we change? No, not unless we want to change and actually hear the alarm bells ringing in our ears. We need to respect our body a lot more. Listen to all those alarm bells in your body. This could be your final wake up call. The alarm bell could be in the form of love handles around the waist, ignored illness warnings, tension headaches, and backaches etc. The body tries to inform in many ways that something is wrong. We need to take cognizance and take remedial steps. The earlier the better! Don't hide behind emotional masks. Do yourself a favour. Don't smile when you are in pain. Don't make an effort to laugh when you wish to cry. As the mind starts listening to you, you become its master—you no longer remain its slave.

Maintain the mental harmony between the mind, body and soul. Even now somewhere those alarm bells must be re-sounding. Listen to them.

## Start a 'Cry Club'

Silly as it may sound; crying releases chemicals from the brain that make us feel better. Be innovative. Start a 'Cry Club.' The idea of a 'laughter club' was sneered at in the beginning, but today worldwide it is helping adults emotionally, more than their throats, every morning. Don't you release your body waste every morning? So what's the harm if you discharge mental garbage through those salty teardrops? Try it. If it works for James Bond, it can work for you as well.

> Remember, it is okay to make mistakes, but it is not okay to live with the pain for ever.

## Listen to your true calling in life

That is a make-believe. Do you want your life to turn into a soap opera? Are you trying to fit the outside world into yours? This is similar to fitting a round peg in a square hole. It's a mistake. The world is too large to fit into your frame.

Being honest about your feelings will be more helpful. Don't get influenced by what the cinema and soap operas show. Try to live life your own way, without submitting to the norms of the external environment. Don't distance yourself from your inner feelings.

My friend's daughter, as a teenager was very clear in her mind that she would be anything but a doctor or an engineer. After she passed her twelfth, she was coerced into taking admission in a prestigious engineering college by her father. Despite being a brilliant child, she could not cope with the pressure of a personally unfulfilling academic pressure. Her grades started falling. Eventually, she came up with the courage to discuss her problem with her parents. Fortunately, her parents were understanding and cooperative enough to help her make a career switch. She proved her mettle and today she is a happy and successful businesswoman. Their son too found his true calling at an early age of seventeen. By this time the parents had learned from their previous mistake. So when the boy wanted to drop out of college and venture out, they decided to give him a chance. He was given one year to prove himself. And it was worth it. The boy is one of the youngest entrepreneurs today.

But how many are allowed to give wings to their passion? Many youngsters are stuck with the lifelong pain of carrying the burden of a profession forced onto them by the circumstances. Some of them may even want to change their names but the horror of the parent's reaction forces them to suppress their true feelings. Over a period of time, frustration leads to unpleasant situations both in personal and professional life. They even forget that they had a passion for something else other than what they have been doing. Being a rebel would mean losing their families, reputation, and cutting off from all relations. Enjoying what one is doing is the cheapest healthy pill to happiness. Mark Twain once said, "Twenty years from now you will be more disappointed by the things you didn't do than by the things you did do."

Remember it is okay to make mistakes, but it is not okay to live with the pain for ever. Releasing pain is not always easy. At times our spirits are too wounded to react. Yet, these are times when we need to release our pain the most.

In the words of Mark Twain, "Throw off the bowlines. Sail away from the safe harbour. Catch the trade winds in your sails." Challenge yourself and understand the feelings. You need to feel, deal, and heal those feelings to accomplish a sense of freedom, peace, and sense of well-being. Let a little steam from the inner emotional pressure cooker be out from time to time. Explore! Dream! Discover! Only then will it result in healthier relationships and a happier and a fulfilling life.

> "There are a few occasions in our lives when we have been angry or lost our tempers, on which we can look back without regret."
>
> (Ashley Montague)

## Anger

Duryodhana's angry reaction to Draupadi's insensitive remark that the son of a blind man has to be blind and Ravana's angry retort to the distorted story narrated by his sister Surpanakha, changed the history of Mahabharata and Ramayana. All of us have heard stories about how even our venerable Rishis used to curse people in anger and then repent. Someone turned into stone and someone else into a parrot. Thank god! No one now has these divine powers; otherwise we would come across millions of miserable and strange creatures hanging around in our residential colonies.

Anger is an emotion which human kind has refined and nurtured over a period of time. Tolerance levels have fallen very low. We get angry on the slightest pretext. We get angry while driving, while eating, while reading newspaper, and while talking to our parents or children. We get angry if the driver is late by a minute and if our junior at office is not laughing at our jokes.

Anger is like drinking poison and then hoping it will kill our enemies. Whereas in reality, it harms the self more than anyone else. Anger affects the emotional tone of the house which affects all members of family. No one wins—everyone loses. The effect of anger on our physical, mental, and spiritual wellness is dangerous. It motivates people to behave in destructive ways. People get angry and kill each other in road rage. There are shoot outs in a moment of anger. I have seen marriages being broken because of anger. I have seen parents crying because of their children's anger. I have known people losing their jobs because of anger. Eventually, anger is related to violence, crime, divorce, spouse, and child abuse, stormy relationships, poor working conditions, poor physical health (migraine, hypertension, and heart attacks), emotional disorders, and the list goes on. No one feels safe around a person full of explosive anger.

Any person who knows the right use of anger is an evolved soul. If someone told you that anger is poisonous and can kill us instantly, would you risk being angry? I'm sure not. We humans tend to treat anger casually because we think it is okay to be angry. What we think as natural behaviour is actually a bad habit we have got so used to that it has become our second nature. Let's stop pretending that it's natural to get angry.

Before we start to discuss the ways and means to deal with anger, let us see how anger works.

> No incident is responsible for anger. It is our response to the situation that creates anger.

## Pharmacology of Anger

People have different ways of expressing anger. Some withdraw into a shell. They cork their anger and let it ferment. Over a period of time it turns into a lasting grudge. For some, anger explodes at the slightest trigger. Some turn red in the face and tremble, while some others use caustic and cutting words.

Whatever way we react to anger—whether we spew it out or keep it inside, it is bound to take a toll on our health. When a person is angry, his body releases epinephrine and norepinephrine hormones which elevate the blood sugar level, increase heart rate, and have a suppressive effect on the immune system. The mind is restless too. Even when the anger subsides, there are unhealthy side effects. Continuous anger in women may result in malignant breast tumours. When we get angry under normal circumstances and forget about it, it leaves less scars. But if we are unable to forget and memory replays the same emotions, it gets painful and harmful.

How anger creeps in, is a debatable issue. Some people believe that anger is a part of our genes. Others hold parents, children, society, and situations responsible for turning them into an angry and foul-mouthed person, thus blaming outside factors for their unhappiness. To me, all these theories are made by intellectuals over a period of great time and immense research, to make people blame someone else for their actions. Oh! I slapped my wife because she provoked me. Oh! I abused the rickshaw puller because he was on the wrong side. By holding people and things outside us responsible for our anger, we are shirking responsibility for our life.

Others do not make us angry (repeat this to yourself as many times before flipping your lid). It is our own thinking that leads to anger. The way we think of the world, the world thinks of us. We experience a mirror image of ourselves in the outside world. Anger is mostly the result of suppressed and repressed emotions. When we hold back anger, we are suppressing it. It results in depression, tiredness, and headache because we do not want to fight. Whereas, when we hold back feelings since childhood, even when we are as young as five years old, it is repression. Anna was twenty-eight when I met her. A very pleasant and educated girl-next-door kind of a girl. She used to work with an architect as his partner. Life was good and she was enjoying it to the fullest. Once a month or so, she used to wake up with severe pain in her right hand. She went to a psychotherapist and during the course of treatment; they came across a fact which was an eye-opener. They realized that when Anna was five years old, her elder sister used to beat her with her plastic doll on her right hand. She was still resentful about it and whenever she remembered it, the pain came back, with a vengeance. The psychotherapist asked her to talk it out with her sister. They met and the elder sister cried her heart out, after realizing the amount of anguish her actions had caused her younger sister. Once Anna realized that her sister did not have any malicious intent, her pain vanished.

That's the danger of being resentful and keeping the anger in your heart. Many people carry repressed anger since childhood when they were vulnerable, tender, and dependent. This results in gastrointestinal, respiratory, circulatory, and skin disorders. Repressed anger is a leading killer of love, joy, health, happiness, loving relationships, family harmony, success, and prosperity—everything that is good and fair. Repressed anger is not caused, as it is already there. It just gets triggered. In a society where about ninety per cent of the families are dysfunctional, a majority of the people have repressed anger. Where there is repressed anger, genuine happiness and peace of mind does not stand a chance.

Nevertheless, let us take care of the beast and not explain away our anger with some theory. Let us see how we can control our anger before it controls us.

## A Healthy Model of Handling Angry Feelings

"To be angry with the right person, to the right degree, at the right time, for the right purpose and in the right way—is not within everybody's power."

(Aristotle)

How effectively we deal with stress, disappointments, and frustration, determines the essence of our personality. Nobody else, but we and only we can free ourselves from anger. We can be our own best therapist, guru, saviour, and teacher . . . if only we pay attention and listen to ourselves.

There are two issues that need to be taken care of: how to prevent or control our own anger and how to handle someone else's aggression against us. This chapter is about self-control. Moreover, a person who can manage his own anger effectively can manage the anger of others as well. Practicing self-control is an important key to handle anger and one can get that only through restrain and continuous practice against regular stress, daily problems, and triggers.

We need to develop our anger management techniques.

## Create a positive environment

Going for an evening walk with one of my friends is a part of my daily routine. On the way, we generally meet an old lady in her late fifties. My friend makes it a point to greet her. What makes it interesting is that the old lady never reciprocates. But despite her unfriendly behaviour, my friend would wish her with the same warmth. One day I couldn't help asking her, "Why don't you stop wishing this *khadoos* old woman?" "Why do I have to let somebody else make the decision about what my actions should be?" replied my friend coolly. I was truly impressed.

No incident is responsible for anger. It is our response to the situation that creates anger. If we squeeze a lemon, we will get sour lemon juice. It is foolish to expect sweet mango juice out of it. What comes out is what is there already inside. Similarly, when we squeeze a person, what comes out depends on what is inside him—love, hate, jealousy, anger . . . Screaming at children means we are either frightening them into silence or making them into future violent adults.

Create a pleasant environment around you and the children. We cannot stop other people's behaviour, but we can have control over our own emotions and behaviour. Unless we discipline our own emotions first, we cannot discipline our children. The best way is to start from changing our inner state and let our emotions be governed by ourselves.

> If you try pushing your mind when you are angry, it will not help. Anger makes us uptight. Learn to relax your body in the moments of anger.

## Accept your anger

Recognizing anger is the first step towards accepting anger. Be aware and recognize your anger when it occurs. Know it is there. Learn to become more aware of what you are feeling at that point of time. Notice the signs that anger is building up (e.g. becoming tense, developing a headache, etc.). Just recognize it. Do not do anything about it. Judging and analysing emotions only compounds the stress. Understanding comes with experience; awareness comes when the effort is made. So have patience and keep the effort on till it becomes a habit.

Once you have acknowledged your anger, just accept it. Maybe write it down so that you do not react. Accepting it does not mean to become a pessimist. We accept it the way it is. You will be pleasantly surprised to see that it slowly disappears. Acceptance is the key to inner alchemy. Denial and pretence leads to disastrous results. Why do some people become sexual perverts? They have harboured wrong feelings about sex. Suppressed feelings result in mental disturbances. This issue is dealt with in detail in the chapter 'Suppressed pains.'

Do not do anything, while the emotion lasts. Now breathe in and breathe out. "Breathing in, I know that I am angry. Breathing out,

I calm my feeling of anger." Just by breathing deeply, we have the power to calm it. We are being mindful of our anger and not suppressing it. Get back to being calm first and then in a very gentle way, tell the person who is making you angry," I would like you to know that I am angry. What you just said hurt me a lot." Just saying that, mindfully and calmly, gives relief. Fix an evening to solve the problem. The time gap is to make the victim and the aggressor receptive to each other's ideas. One person looking at the roots of your suffering is good, two people looking at it is even better.

## Learn to challenge your anger

"Any person capable of angering you becomes your master. He can make you angry only when you permit yourself to be disturbed by him."

(Epictetus, Roman philosopher)

Most of us are educated enough to differentiate between right and wrong, good and evil. We are also capable of recognizing an inadequacy in ourselves and reshape our personality. Challenge the hidden fear behind anger by allowing yourself to feel it fully. And while you are feeling it fully, choose not to act in anger. This way, we challenge our anger. "I know you, I feel you, I feel your power on me but I will not allow you to take charge of my mind and soul." To do this, we need to use our will power. I remember a friend who used to be sexually harassed by her male colleague on a regular basis. She was tired of him but also wanted him to know that he had no control over her. So every time he made a crude remark, she just looked at him, the way someone looks through a glass pane. The guy did not change and he got more aggressive, to an extent, of saying things in front of other colleagues. One day, in an office party, where all the senior officers and their wives were present, he made the mistake of making some comment which had sexual connotations. My friend had trained herself to ignore him and to look through him but not the other colleagues and their wives. He was asked to leave his job, then and there by the CEO, in front of three hundred people. That's the power of enjoying your anger. Make him your servant and not the other way around.

When we challenge the anger, we are giving ourselves a chance to control it. When we choose not to get angry, we are allowing ourselves to remain balanced.

## Watch Your Body Language

Carl Rogers believed that our feelings, thinking, and physical set [musculature, posture, and facial expressions] are closely related.

Whenever I had a fight with my husband, I used to control my anger and make it a non-serious issue. But when I used to go out with him to the parties after the fight, my body language and my posture would give me away. I would be taut and uncomfortable in my own skin. People who see us every day can figure out that something is not right. Others may perceive our body language as snobbish or arrogant.

Take care of the body and the mind will follow automatically. Most people start with the mind and they fail. They fail because they start from the wrong place. You can't teach a child history before you teach him the alphabets. Everything should be done in a right order. If you try pushing your mind when you are angry, it will not help. Anger makes us uptight. Learn to relax your body in the moments of anger. When we no longer feel wound up inside, we can adjust better from the outside. Loosen up by walking. Listen to the body. Deliberately unclench your fists, drop your shoulders, take a deep breath and let your jaws sag. You will find it relaxing. Listen to music. Jog in the park or go to the gym and punch a bag. Take out your anger on your pillow. This will make you feel better. When the body relaxes, the mind starts to become responsive.

Move systematically: first the simplest step, then the complex, and then the more complex.

> There is always some space between the feelings of anger and the response towards it. We can use this space as a powerful tool to keep our anger in control.

## Respond, Don't React

Imagine a girl who teases you, on a regular basis. She teases you when you are sleeping and teases you when you are reading the newspaper. Will you, in anger, cut off her nose? I don't think so. Then let me ask you this. Why did Laxman cut off Surpanakha's nose, which in a way started the great epic Ramayana? Trust me, there are still many Laxmans in our society who have no control over their emotions. Open up a newspaper and you will see that someone has thrown acid on somebody's face. Somebody has cut someone's body part. Someone has burnt somebody. All this is reaction, not action. Someone is a manipulator and you are the one who is manipulated. He has pushed a button and you have functioned like a machine. That's what people are doing to you: they turn you on, they turn you off. Somebody comes and puffs up our ego, and you feel great; and then somebody comes and punctures it, and you are simply flat on the ground. You are not your own master.

Buddha's reaction to anger is one shining example. "Buddha [was] passing through a village. Some people [were] angry, very much against his teachings. They [abused] him, they [insulted] him. Buddha [listened] silently and then [said], 'If you are finished, then allow me to move on. I have to reach the next village, and they will be waiting for me. If something is still remaining in your mind, then when I am passing back by this route, you can finish it.'

"They [said], 'We have abused you, insulted you. Are you not going to answer?'

"Buddha [said], 'I never react now. What you do is up to you . . . You can abuse me; that is up to you—I am not a slave. I have become a free man.'" (*Awareness*, Osho)

Such is the power of having control over our reactions.

> Compliments work wonders in the heat of battle.

## Stand on the High Ground

A father and son were travelling by a local bus. The father asked the conductor for directions to a certain place. The conductor was quite rude and insulting. The father was unaffected. But the son being young was not happy as he expected his father to retaliate. So when the son asked his father as to why he did nothing, the father replied, "Son, he was rude because it's his nature. He has probably lived with that nature for years. I am mature enough to tolerate it for a minute or two. Son, it means that we should not sink to the level of a person who insults us. Stay on the high ground, where the stones cannot hurt us. When we are angry, arrogant, or high, our words are like non-returnable arrows." The father was none other than Lal Bahadur Shastri.

One of the biggest mistakes we can make is by counter-attacking. Our natural impulse is to lash out and try to prove how wrong our opponent is. We need to resist our mind to start giving justifications and clarifications. The moment the other person sees that he is being understood and his views and opinions are respected, he becomes receptive to our point of view. In this manner, both can emerge victorious.

A boss once sniggered at his junior, "This report stinks. Did you work on it or were you daydreaming?" Anyone would have retaliated with a smart comment. But she said, "I would really appreciate it, if you could tell me as to what you did not like and how exactly you would like the report to be? I have been writing reports for twelve years now and nobody has analysed it so critically." The boss was quiet for a moment and realized his mistake. He apologized to her and told that he was angry because he was in the middle of long and messy divorce. That incident brought them together and they became the best of friends. Today they are happily married.

Tactfully handling anger elicits better response. My friend who hates noisy roads once asked the autodriver not to honk. He did it despite the request. She simply said, "If you do it again, you will become a sinner. God does not advocate honking." The ploy worked once. It did not cut ice another time. When it did not, she said to the driver, "Honking constantly will make you deaf." That worked. She now enjoys discovering new fenders when she meets with pesky drivers who honk relentlessly.

## What else can we do?

More than saying the right thing, higher wisdom is required to not to say the wrong thing in anger. There is always some space between the feelings of anger and the response towards it. We can use this space as a powerful tool to keep our anger in control. Catch that moment and hold on to it. With the help of the techniques below, we can widen this space and use it to our advantage.

- Count up to ten before reacting.
- Give the 'Provoker' the Benefit of Doubt: Instead of inflaming our anger by feeding ourselves with such thoughts as "Who does he think he is for treating me like

this?" we can suggest to ourselves that perhaps this man has had a bad day. Come up with a reasonable justification for his behaviour that you can relate to.

- Compliments work wonders in the heat of battle. Say something positive about that person who is abusing you. "You have been such an understanding person. There has to be something really annoying, otherwise you are not one to get worked up so easily." Watch his temperature come down from hundred to zero.

- Forgive the person. Do not mistake it for weakness. A weak person cannot forgive; forgiveness is the attribute of the strong.

Remember, for every ten minutes of anger, we lose six hundred seconds of happiness. Less anger obviously means more happiness. Annoying things will keep happening; people will keep making you angry. Keep on working on it relentlessly as overcoming anger is an ongoing process.

*"If we could sell our worrying hours for what they cost us, we would all have been millionaires."*

(Anonymous)

Worry

Four people were on a plane; a pilot, a politician, a teacher, and a student. Mid-air, the pilot announced, "Something is wrong with the aircraft. There are only three parachutes and I am an important person . . ." he took one parachute and jumped out. The politician hearing this, hurriedly said, "I am also an important person . . ." he took another and jumped out. The teacher advised the student, "I have lived my life. You take the last parachute and save yourself." The student said, "Master, there are still two more parachutes and both of us can be saved." The teacher exclaimed, "How can that be! Two have already jumped out. Hence there must be only one parachute." The student answered, "Master, the politician was so worried and in such a hurry, that he took my school bag and jumped." (*Looking at Life Differently* by Swami Sukhabodhananda)

Being worried and tensed is reason enough to be ineffective. Although a little amount of worry is acceptable and healthy too but when people take it to extremes, it results in jeopardizing their mental makeup. Some people worry to death about the negative possibilities in their lives and become paragons of unfounded misfortunes.

In our daily activities, over-worrying leads to loss of focus. Some people unnecessarily worry about their unpaid bills, or their job security, or about their children and their studies, careers, etc. Most often, parents nudge their children 'Study or you will fail.' Another common worry game is, "When will you start worrying about your future?" No matter how much children tell mothers to take a chill pill, it does not diffuse the worrisome situation. The result? They lose confidence, have disturbed sleep, become obsessive, get 'butterflies' in their stomachs frequently, and always look emotionally drained because of their worrying nature. How can such people ever be happy?

> Most of the times we worry, fret, and stew over things that never happen.

The funny thing about worry is that most of the times we worry, fret, and stew over things that never happen. I remember my mother pacing up and down whenever my brother was out with his friends. She would get all sorts of worrisome thoughts and would not sleep. When I look back, I feel sorry for her having spent half of her life worrying about baseless misfortunes. Same way, one of my cousins was a paratrooper. My aunt spent her whole life worrying about his parachute jumps. Nothing happened. But the very first day back home, he tripped over a stone and broke his rib which she had never worried about.

So worrying is nothing but one sure way of deteriorating the quality of life. Living in the past or thinking about the future takes us nowhere. It is only in the present moment that we can learn, develop and grow.

Is the phantom of worry stalking you too?

## Hold your worry horses!

In an answer to the question whether the Civil War was necessary, Abraham Lincoln supposedly told an anecdote to Horace Greeley. In his circuit riding days, Lincoln and his companions, riding to the next session of court, had crossed many swollen rivers. But the Fox River was still ahead of them; and they said to each other, "If these streams give us so much trouble, how shall we get over Fox River?"

When darkness fell, they stopped for the night at a lodging place, where they met the Methodist presiding elder of the district who rode through the country in all kinds of weather and knew all about the Fox River. They gathered around him and asked him about the present state of the river. "Oh, yes," replied the circuit rider, "I know all about the Fox River. I have crossed it often and understand it well. But I have one fixed rule with regard to Fox River: I never cross it till I reach it." (McCartney)

The moral of the story is: 'Don't worry and wrestle with problems before they are really problems.' What a good advice for us all!

## Develop a positive attitude

Do you look at a glass with little water and say, "The glass is half empty," or do you think "it's half full"? Your outlook in life will determine your answer. If you are a positive person, the glass will seem half full. If you are a negative person, the glass will be half empty. Most parents fret over getting children to study, earn, get married, and look after themselves! Well it's a huge responsibility. But some parents make too serious an agenda out of it. I remember I came second in my eighth standard. I reached home happy and excited. The moment I saw my mother, I screamed "Maa, I am second in the class!" "But why not first?" frowned my mother. Imagine how I must have felt as a child! All my happiness and excitement fizzled out. Sometimes such an attitude can create a permanent dent in relationships.

Instead, why not enjoy the current situation? If you don't have a child, enjoy other aspects of a blissful marriage. Once you are blessed with a child, don't start fretting over her future, and rather enjoy her childhood. Make the best of the situation you are in. A ship was moving and a huge crocodile attacked it. People started throwing things in his mouth—chairs, tables, a bag of oranges, and finally a Jew. But this did not stop the crocodile. It came back again. Finally it was caught and its belly cut open. To every one's utter surprise the Jew was seen sitting on a chair, selling oranges to people swallowed by the crocodile before. Well, what a positive person!

Do not exaggerate the problem. Be happy and blessed that you never got the worse. My friend met with an accident on a busy street in Mumbai. Guess what? She fractured her ankle, tore her ligaments, and dislocated her knee. But she was glad that it happened on only one leg. She thanked God that the other leg was okay. How many of us can think like that?

## Laughter—a great stress buster

William James, the father of modern psychology, said, "We don't laugh because we are happy. We are happy because we laugh."

If you don't have wrinkles, you have not laughed enough. The famous beautician Helena Rubenstein said, "A few wrinkles as we grow older, are not undesirable. They are part and parcel of the character of your face. Without them the face is like an empty book. But they must be the right kind of lines, like the laughter lines or the impressions formed on face by a smile. They should be narrating a happy story of a beautiful past and a bright future." Do you know laughing one hundred times is equal to a ten-minute workout on a rowing machine? Laughter helps promote healing in the body by lowering blood pressure and increasing blood flow. It releases the negative emotions and makes one feel better. Laughter according to Norman Cousins, is a kind of 'internal jogging' that can be even more health restoring than the external kind. Norman had "laughed himself out of" a collagen disease that a whole battery of experts couldn't cure. His recovery from this disease by watching humorous cartoons is well-documented.

> Accepting a little dust in life can save us from a lot of frustrations. When we lower our standards, our stress level comes down automatically.

One of my late cousin brothers, Rajender bhai, was a clerk in a school. Unfortunately, he got suspended for no fault of his. His suspension lasted for almost two years. It was one of the most difficult phases of his life as he did not get his salary during this period. One day when he visited us, I enquired how he was managing. His answer was a classic one. He said, *"Jiji, yeh Bhagwan bhi maanega nahi. Woh mujhe lakhpati banaake hi rahega."* (God is hell-bent on making me a millionaire!). I wondered what he meant. He continued, "You see, the day I win the case, which I have no doubt about, I'll get the lump sum in lacs. And that day I will become a LAKHPATI . . . ha ha ha!" He laughed. Any other person in his place would have cracked up, but his sense of humour kept him going through tough times. Such a simple solution to control the worrying habit! Yet the research says that on an average, a four-year-old laughs about three hundred times a day, whereas an adult laughs about fifteen times a day only. It's never too late if we start making a conscious effort to laugh more from this moment itself. Join the laughter club.

## Accept imperfections in life

Some people end up doing everything themselves as they are unable to trust that others will do an equally good job. They don't realize that the jobs they delegate to others are being done with individual levels of perfection. We don't live in a perfect world. Too much of perfection lands one on the clinic couch. So what does one do? Well, accepting a little dust in life can save us from a lot of frustrations. When we lower our standards, our stress level comes down automatically. Try it.

## Allot yourself a specific time to worry

If you can't help worrying about something, don't waste your whole day worrying about it. Set aside a specific time to worry. Wallow, cry, howl, read an inspirational book, share it with your dear ones, or worry in silence—whatever way it suits you. Don't fret 24 x 7 over it. Train yourself to leave your problem behind, the moment that period ends. This simple but powerful technique is helpful in reducing the time we spend worrying. Eventually, it serves to eliminate the habit forever.

## Empty your mental garbage on a regular basis

The mind is like a land. We can make it fertile with good thoughts or make it barren with negativity or bad feelings. Being humans, we may initially find it difficult to stop our mind from filling itself with mental garbage. So one more technique is—'empty the garbage every night.' Discard every night the little worries, jealousies, anger, and resentment that get accumulated during the day. Even better, empty it three to four times a day. This is another tale worth pondering over:

Two monks were travelling in the rain, mud sloshing under their feet. Suddenly they saw a beautiful finely dressed girl unable to cross the river. Without a word, the older monk picked up the girl and carried her to the other side of the river. Agitated and disgusted, the younger monk exploded at him after reaching the destination. "How could you, a monk, even consider holding a woman in your arms, that too a young and beautiful one? It is so much against our teachings."

"I put her down at the roadside," said the older monk. "Are you still carrying her?"

We all 'carry her' for years and decades and become stressful. Why not start having self-audit sessions and throw thousands of 'hers' into the dustbin?

## Make your life simpler

Most of us have the tendency to store junk in the house which leaves no space for new things. A lot of stress comes from doing things we don't want to. As per Feng Shui, clutter is nothing but stuck energy. Similarly, we have a lot of emotional garbage stored inside us which keeps us stuck in unhealthy and undesirable life patterns. To sort out our lives, we need to sort out the junk first.

Keep life simple by minimizing the demands of life as well as maintaining a level of comfort. Simplifying is all about having enough and not too much. For some, it may mean shifting to a smaller house or buying a smaller car. For some others, it may mean letting go of some stressful relationships, and for some, cleaning out unused junk and crammed cupboards. Author Jerome K Jerome once said, "Let your boat of life be light, packed with only what you need—a homely home and simple pleasures, one or two friends, worth the name, someone to love and someone to love you, a cat, a dog, and a pipe or two, enough to eat and enough to wear, and a little more than enough to drink; for thirst is a dangerous thing."

I appreciate my husband's desire to have a farmhouse. But of late, I have been against the idea. The reason is simple. It requires a lot of time and energy to maintain a farmhouse which we lack at this age. I have no desire to increase our blood pressure and ruin our happiness. Same way, I have brought the interiors of my house down to minimal. The house looks spacious, not much room for insects and easy to manage and maintain. Less stress and more happiness! Take an honest look at your life. Be sure that everything you hang onto, are things that you specifically choose to have around. Take control of the things you bring into your life and you will have a much happier existence. Learn to ask 'why' to yourself. Why do I want to go on a cruise? Why do I need this new model of a car? Do these things contribute to my life and my potential for enjoyment and satisfaction or I am doing it to impress others? Consider each influence and ask yourself: 'Should I discard it or give it more of my energy?' When you get the answers you will automatically start eliminating the clutter—the stress from life. It will help you in taking the decision to let go.

> Keep life simple by minimizing the demands of life as well as maintaining a level of comfort.

## Watch your thoughts

Descartes declared once, "I think therefore I am."

This shows the importance of thinking and choosing the right words. What we think, speak, and act with people in everyday life, has a profound impact on what we are and the quality of life we are leading. Somebody has wisely said:

Watch your thoughts, they become your words.

Watch your words, they become your actions.

Watch your actions, they become your habits.

Watch your habits, they become your character.

Happiness is like a harvest; stress is like weeds. Tilling, seeding, watering, fertilizing, and weeding are essential to get a good yield; else we are bound to get nothing but weeds. Start your day with a feeling of love and happiness. The first thirty minutes after waking usually determine our mood and how the day will go. So make sure these golden waking minutes are full of pleasure. Start the morning with positive thoughts. Think of the fun and the way you will pick up the challenges of the day with staff, friends, strangers, and family members. Do anything that will enlighten your soul. Say a prayer, write a poem, paint a picture—anything you like. Spend some time in an old age home or an orphanage and see how blessed you feel. Find out what is polluting your mind. Destroy toxic thoughts before they destroy you. This mental dry-cleaning can become a precursor to good habits and a fabulous character.

## Balance your life

Balancing our lives is like rope walking. If not balanced properly, there is a danger of toppling over. You can never be exactly in the middle for any length of time. Similarly, things can never be right all the time. Enjoy and be happy in happy times. Be sad in sad moments. Don't deny them. If they have to happen, they will anyway happen. Take life as it comes. Learn to accept the situations that life throws up. Do not resist.

## Count your blessings

Be grateful to God. He has given this wonderful existence to us to enjoy. Let's not take our fortunes for granted. Let us count our blessings, and acknowledge all the happiness we have.

Here is something you might have read quite often.

> Count your blessings instead of your crosses;
> Count your gains instead of your losses.
> Count your joys instead of your woes;
> Count your friends instead of your foes.
> Count your smiles instead of your tears;
> Count your courage instead of your fears.
> Count your full years instead of your lean;
> Count your kind deeds instead of your mean.
> Count your health instead of your wealth . . .

Make some principles to live by every day. At the end of a good day thank the Lord for helping you to get through. Be grateful to all those who have helped you to complete the day without any mishap. Soon this will become a ritual.

Nothing happens overnight. You will still get the tug in the middle of night 'Get up. Let's worry.' It is up to you to say 'yes' or 'no.' The choice is yours.

# PART TWO

# Intervention Strategies for the Persistent Defeatist Attitude

Issues that have been discussed so far are bound to be helpful in evaluating various aspects of our lives. Once we have understood who is pulling our emotional strings, we can take stock. Once we know our energy leaks and how to limit them, we can start working on optimizing our energy consumption. We have the best chance to develop new habits. The old ones will just float away.

Nonetheless, old habits die hard. They persist for a variety of reasons. Important in those reasons are the explanations and excuses we give in our defence. The most common amongst these are:

## 'I have no choice'

The belief that 'I am helpless and can't do anything about my situation' is a common rationale for doing nothing. It is a powerful preventative to change and happiness.

## 'I better overlook'

To overlook is a way of being 'unaware.' By overlooking, we deny parts of reality that are unpleasant and unsatisfying. For example, sometimes we overlook a nasty remark and pretend not to be angry when actually we are very angry. This attitude takes away our freedom to understand and go deep into the psychology of anger. We live and die with anger.

## 'It isn't my fault'

It is another way of 'getting away from responsibility.' We claim to be a victim. Somebody else is responsible for our misfortune and unhappiness. As long as it isn't our fault, there is nothing in our behaviour we need to look at or understand.

Once we awaken to this information, we are ready to take the next step. Those who still have the defeatist attitude need to put in a little more to build a strong foundation. If we really want to change, we need to understand why some of our behaviour is still resistant or persistent. Understanding resistance gives us clarity of mind—why we have been so enduring to some of our behaviours which we know should have been discarded long back. To beat the subconscious at its own game, we need to explore other intervention strategies. Each step in the right direction will get us new rewards and closer to our goal.

"The man of awareness lives in light.
He is egoless and a delight.
Need not stumble, grope, or fight."

(Kabir)

## Bring Awareness in Life

Vedic society in India was very happy and probably that's why it was known as Satyuga. The story goes that when people started to exploit the benefits of happiness in ancient times, Lord Brahma decided to hide happiness. Many hiding places were suggested in the celestial world, like the dark recess of the earth or sinking it into the deep ocean. It was then that Lord Brahma ultimately resolved to hide happiness within the soul of man. He reasoned, "No man will ever think of looking within himself, so it will be difficult to find it." How true! Centuries have passed. Generations of humanity have been reborn in birth and death. Everyone looks for peace and happiness in all places except in the self.

Happiness is completely an inside job. We need to reach inward, not outward. All the answers lie in our inner self—if we would just listen. And unless we are aware, we can neither listen nor change. Awareness is the key. Those who live life with awareness enjoy freedom and those who act without awareness live a life of bondage. Unfortunately, people are under the wrong impression that they are fully aware of their actions and are doing their best in the given circumstances. They can see a lack of awareness in others, not in themselves. They hold external factors responsible for their unhappiness; resign themselves to their fate, and do nothing to improve the quality of their lives.

I read a story once. Drunk out of his wits, a man staggered in a graveyard. In the dark, he slipped and fell in a burial hole. He was so sloshed, that he fell asleep. A few minutes later, another drunk trotted by and created a scene in the graveyard—loud enough to wake up the drunkard. He got up and feeling a wee bit cold, shouted, "Hey, I am feeling cold". The drunk outside the hole strained his eyes and wondered how the body got up! Nevertheless in his unconscious state he said, "Hey, you have removed all the soil. No wonder you are cold." They both go on to sleep, blissfully unaware of their surroundings.

A person who knows that he knows not, has a chance to work on his 'knows not' areas. But a person who knows not that he knows not, has hardly anything to work on.

Reacting to anger, living in the past, negative attitudes, unwarranted worries . . . all that which take us away from happiness is the result of a lack of awareness. The chain of self-defeating behaviour develops right through childhood and continues till the end. Eventually, we reproach ourselves rather than seeking proper, healthy solutions. We pay a very heavy price for the lack of awareness in life. It is due to our lack of awareness that we overlook the signals our body sends. Lack of attention to a simple cold turns it into pneumonia; negligence to a simple eye problem can cost us our eyes. If we control our emotions and do not totally mourn the death of a loved one, emotional congestion can turn into panic attacks or lung problems. In a state of unhappiness and unawareness, many start to drown themselves in alcoholism, gambling, smoking, or other vices. Instead of alleviating the anxiety, it only propels the problem further and leads to problems in relationships, survival issues, professional hazards, etc. Only when it hits us badly, do we take a note of it.

Socrates said, "Know thyself," and declared that the unexamined life is not worth living.

> A person who knows that he knows not, has a chance to work on his 'knows not' areas. But a person who knows not that he knows not, has hardly anything to work on.

## The magic of knowing who we are

*Kuhn states that "awareness is prerequisite to all acceptable changes of theory."*

False assumptions and beliefs ignite our emotional reactions. Whether it's changing the false beliefs, controlling the emotional reactions, developing will power, or gaining any kind of self-mastery over issues obstructing our dealing and healing, self-awareness is the key to change and lasting happiness. The first step in changing the way we create our life is self-awareness. We cannot expect to change what we are not aware of. It is the means to identify our unconscious patterns and raise them in our consciousness.

Awareness brings clarity of mind and allows us to perceive the present reality. When we are aware, we view things differently. We analyse things in an honest and non-judgmental way. Self-awareness makes it easier for us to identify our contribution in a troubled relationship. We will be shocked with revelations about ourselves and the people in our lives, if only we take time out and put in a little effort in the direction of awareness. When we know how and where we are playing a part in the upsets, we are ready to take responsibility for what has taken place, which in turn helps us to take appropriate actions. Self-awareness is all about facing the truth—the real us. We keep on fooling ourselves in the absence of awareness, not in its presence.

Self-awareness is a very useful tool to understand our thinking pattern. We can discard the unwarranted feelings and behaviour—the product of the limited self—with the help of awareness, thus making space for more useful ones. It gives control over false beliefs, which in turn save us from spending our energy on reacting rather than acting. Anything that is taking us away from happiness can be overpowered in the state of awareness. This energy can be stored and used to break away from other self-defeating habits. It is a tool to increase personal power in all areas of life. This in turn enhances our relationship with others. Wake up from the slumber! Awaken the Buddha in you.

> We will be shocked with revelations about ourselves and the people in our lives, if only we take time out and put in a little effort in the direction of awareness.

## Watch your life

A king, after having woken up from his afternoon nap, told his minister that just a moment back he saw himself as a butterfly. Now, he finds himself as a king. Which one is true? The minister tried to convince him that he was a not a butterfly but a king. But the king was not convinced. He said, "How do you know which one was a dream? Maybe at this moment, I am a butterfly dreaming that I am a king."

It is only in the moments of awareness that we can awaken ourselves from the eternal slumber and put an end to all confusions.

Marilyn Voss Savant says about life:

"To acquire knowledge, one must study;
But to acquire wisdom, one must observe."

Observing can only happen when we are aware. When we listen to our own voice of reason rather than other's voices, we become wise. We will know our true identity only with self-awareness. Or else we will spend our life like the eaglet that grew with the chickens and lived like one.

In a farmhouse lived many hens. In a bunch of eggs laid by one hen, fell an eagle's egg. When the eggs hatched, among the chickens an eaglet was also born. The eaglet believed itself to be a chicken as it was born with other chickens. It grew up amongst the chickens and became just like them. It learnt to cluck, make noises and flapped its wings. It also learnt to fly like the other chicks. As time passed by, the eaglet grew bigger. One day it saw in the sky a beautiful creature soaring in the horizon. Amazed at how high it could fly, the eaglet asked the hen what was that creature, flying so elegantly? The hen said, "Oh that's an eagle, king of all flying birds. It lives in the clouds while we live on earth." Since the young eagle had resigned to its fate, even when he learnt about the amazing eagle he could do nothing. He lived like a chicken and died like one. Had he been aware of his true identity, his life would have been much blessed! (*Stop sleepwalking through life* by Devdas Menon)

Most of the people I meet during my evening walks are talking on their mobile phones. Some carry iPods when they walk. They walk like robots, depriving themselves of the sounds and music around. They miss out on the greenery and the beauty of nature. There is this gentleman—an exception—whom I find admiring nature, talking to birds, inhaling oxygen, and embracing each moment as he walks. His sense of awareness is distinctly visible through his smile. This is awareness—to be fully present in whatever we are doing.

Simply observe things that you do every day. Learn to do one thing at a time and give it your complete attention. When you are chopping vegetables and stirring them while cooking, feel the movements of your arms. Listen to the crackling sound of spices as you put them in ghee/oil and inhale the aroma. Experience the joy of cooking. If you are washing clothes, focus on the movements of your hands, the scrubbing, the water, the dirt coming out of the clothes— everything connected to the washing process. Do every act with as much awareness as possible. The same goes for the traffic inside the mind. Most of us have experienced or caused embarrassment when in conversation with others. We nod our heads but don't remember what the other person said. The other day I met one of my old friends. She asked me, "Where is your daughter?" I told her that she was in Bombay. After a few minutes, she repeated the same question. I understood that her mind was elsewhere. Not hearing does not necessarily mean that the person is not interested in you. It happens when our mind is busy working in too many directions. Learn to direct your attention consciously.

> With the master key of awareness we can eliminate the unwanted elements like anger, jealousy, fear, and pain.

Take a document, any document, and practice reading it through without letting your mind wander. Be conscious. Observe your thoughts. Sit still in your office chair for two minutes. Even while you are sitting quietly in a train or plane just close your eyes. Feel your emotions. When we simply acknowledge the thoughts and let them just pass through the mind, they lose power over us. Slowly, as awareness sets in, our perceptions clear like the mist on a cold morning. It makes it possible for us to be comfortable with 'what is.' It brings acceptance, flexibility, and compassion into the inevitable. That makes space for us to deal with the problem with an open mind. Don't worry when you are distracted. Be determined and keep bringing your focus back with each distraction, till awareness becomes your guide and you become the master of your thoughts.

Sometimes it is not the effort and hard work that is important, simple act of being alert changes equations. See yourself changing and feel the change. Zero-in on the problems that irritate and make you feel angry and out of control.

**Be aware of:**

- Things which exhaust your senses and virtually make you go into a tailspin.
- Things which motivate your creativity and bring out the best in you.

When we act with awareness we don't make too many mistakes. Think hard and deep and you will find out what is in your mind. Don't try to control what is going wrong. You will only drive yourself out of your mind. Instead of controlling your worry just become aware of what's driving you towards it? When we are aware, negativity will not hound us. We become positive. It is like when you switch on the lights in the house at night, darkness disappears. So is the case with our thoughts. Bad thoughts vanish in the light of awareness. When we are aware, we can still get angry and not be affected by it.

There is a popular story that goes like this. An incorrigible thief decided it was high time he had a spiritual master. So he approached a learned one in his city and told the master to make him his disciple. The thief also had a condition that the master should not ask him to leave his core business. The placid guru heeded the request. But he told the disciple that he too had a condition. That he could burgle as much he liked but he should do it with awareness. Without thinking the thief agreed to his master's request. The master said, "When you break into a house, be alert, steal whatever you like. That is not my concern. But just be aware."

119

A few weeks later the thief returned to his master accusing him of tricking him. He said, "When I become aware, I cannot steal. If I steal, awareness disappears. I am confused!" The master said, "I am not concerned with it, it is your problem. Do you want awareness or not?" Since the thief had tasted the joy of awareness, he gave up his profession and turned a new leaf.

Only when you leave your house unattended, it is most likely to be burgled. When the lights are on and everyone in the house is awake, no thief enters. Does it ring a bell? Guard your unwarranted thoughts by being aware. Unwanted thoughts are like fake diamonds, treasured till identified as fake. Once discovered, they lose their importance. Awareness yields huge returns. With the master key of awareness we can eliminate the unwanted elements like anger, jealousy, fear, and pain. Instead of using our energies in negativity, we can use it for awakening the soul.

With awareness, life is no longer a rat race but a pleasant morning walk. To be conscious or to remain unconscious is a choice only we can make. To be aware of the prejudices we have created, we should not hesitate to take help from close family and friends if need be. Look deep within yourself, find the reservoir of peace, and surprise Lord Brahma!

> "It is our choices that show what we truly are,
> far more than our abilities."
>
> (Professor Dumbledore's maxim in J. K. Rowling's
> *Harry Potter and the Chamber of Secrets*)

# Make Conscious Choices

William Jefferson Clinton is believed to have met John F. Kennedy in his teens. He was so impressed by him that he decided that one day he too would become the president of that country. He worked on it. And one day his decision became reality. It brought him a lot of honour and glory. Unfortunately, the same cannot be said of the choice he made to get involved with intern Monica Lewinsky. That regretful decision cost him dearly. Such is the power of choice!

Great people do not stumble over opportunities. It is not chance but their well-thought choices that give them an edge over the others. The choices we make decide whether we will pay or get paid. A choice has always been a precursor to change—whether it happens consciously or unconsciously. Choices can take one to towering heights or plunge in total despair. On both the occasions, the president had a choice. One brought him to fame and the other led him to shame.

When things go wrong, one tends to think of incompetence and bad luck. It is natural. But once the bad mood passes off, think with a rational mind. We are not unlucky all the time; we make some really bad choices for ourselves. Failure or success—it all goes down to our choices and decisions. Each time we take a decision and become unhappy, we need to analyse our choices and see where we have gone wrong. Otherwise, as is rightly said, "If you keep on doing what you've always done, you'll keep getting what you have always got." (W. L. Bateman)

## Unconscious choices

Aware or unaware, we all make choices every moment. Do we get out of bed immediately or push the snooze button? Do we prepare for work or call in sick? Do we watch a cricket match or study? At the job, do we work hard or spend most of our time in the canteen? Throughout the day we continue to make choices to decide what to do next. Sometimes we feel things have gone out of control. This happens when we make wrong choices, even if it is done unconsciously. It is important to understand that most of the times it is our unconscious choices that are responsible for most of our goof-ups and unhappiness. We all consciously think the best for our careers, plan our marriages and retirement. Some of us go to the extent of researching and analysing. Some even take the help of consultants. But what we do not give importance to is, the choices we make each moment.

An unconscious choice is a reaction. It elicits anger, jealously, vengefulness, or fear in a person. We saw a film in the evening and came out of the theatre discussing the plus and minus points of the film. The discussion got so heated that one of us turned away in disgust. We all reached home sulking, brooding, and forgetting that we had enjoyed the movie together a little while ago. We forgot that the movie is make-believe and not worth sulking over. Similarly, there are couples and families fighting over soap operas, matches, games, silly conversations, etc. A perfectly enjoyable evening goes right out of the window. But we still get into animated conversations like this.

Living a life of unconscious choices is like drifting in a boat with the current, without knowing that there is a motor that can be used to take control of the course. Our motor of life is our power of choice. Choose tension or peace, health or sickness, happiness or unhappiness, fear or freedom—anything! You can choose even Heaven! Such is the power of taking conscious decisions.

Like Mahatma Gandhi had his experiments with truth, we all can experiment with life by making conscious choices on a daily basis.

> The choices we make decide
> whether we will pay or get paid.

## How to make a conscious choice?

Empowerment is, seeing reality as it really is; owning the choices we have and making the best of it. There is incredible power in the simple words, 'I choose.' Educator and author Leo Buscaglia stresses the importance of our power to choose this way: "It's time people tell you, you're not at the mercy of forces greater than yourself. You are, indeed, the greatest force for you."

There are some people who bring out the best in them even in the face of tragedies just by choosing differently. Sudha Chandran, the dancer and actor is a great example in our society. She lost her leg in an accident but continues to dance. Her conscious choice not to get bogged down by her personal tragedy, has made her a role model for many. The courage to choose wisely reveals that we are living a proactive, well-thought-out life rather than simply living a reactionary life. Moreover when we make conscious choices, we become a creator and the concept of good and bad luck becomes inconsequential.

The problem is that we do not want to come out of our comfort zones. Yet, unfortunately, there is no other way out to deal with the issue. Every day we will be faced with the maid coming late to work. Every day we will yell, spoil our mood, and go to work unhappily. For a change, finish the work or sack her. Let her know she is not indispensable. Similarly, at work, if you encounter problems, find out where things are going wrong; discover new ways to tackle them and make a change in your choices.

If you catch yourself in the middle of a habitual negative behaviour, say no to it. Even better than saying 'No' to the negative is, saying 'Yes' to the positive. It helps greatly! Here is an incident I would like to share:

One of our friends is a highly egoist couple. Their daughter had an inter-caste marriage, despite stiff resistance from parents. The parents could not reconcile to the fact that their daughter could defy them. They banned her entry in the house. Soon, she was blessed with twin daughters. But the situation did not change. More than the girl, I used to pity the parents who were depriving themselves and their grandchildren of all the fun and pleasure they could have had together. Every time we met, they would rave and rant about how their daughter had let them down and how miserable they felt. One day after having listened to their usual cribbing about how unfair life had been to them, I couldn't help saying, "Don't you think it's you who have chosen this misery?" They were quite upset with my statement. Next day, I received a call from my friend. "Nirmal," she sounded hurt. "How can you be so callous? Our only child betrays us and you say it's our choice!" I said, "Tulika, I fully empathize with what happened to you four years back. But how long do you want to remain miserable is your choice. Isn't it?" After a week, I was pleasantly surprised to see her at my place beaming with happiness with two little bundles of joy.

## Where there is a strong will, there is a choice!

All our news channels are filled up with some kind of story or event about some or the other person. Now, whether the person is in the news for a good or a bad reason is a different issue. What is important is that people who make or break the news are the people who dared to make a choice. Ask all the women who became Miss India, Miss Universe, or Miss World, the secret of their success. The answer is the same: will power. So when you are watching the evening news or reading about any event in a magazine or book, keep in mind that all these events—independent from one another—occurred only after someone had the will to choose them to be so. At the same time there are people like you and me who may not be in the limelight, but they too are making choices every day and every moment. And they too are responsible for the kind of life they are living today—happy or unhappy.

Let us not act as if we are in a rudderless boat drifting in the sea of life. Let us not accept the place where the currents and tides guide us. The boat we are in has a rudder—'the will to choose'! It will steer us where we want to be.

> The courage to choose wisely reveals that we are living a proactive, well-thought-out life rather than simply living a reactionary life.

## Be aware of temptations

In order to get temporary relief, we give in to our temptations. That moment of weakness can become a lifetime of regret. It happens because our threshold for inconvenience is very low. At that moment we do not take into consideration the long term consequences such as unwanted pregnancy, out-of-control debt, or becoming an alcoholic. Some smoke, some drink; some are addicted to phones, some are glued to the television; some are doing drugs, some are gambling; all because they succumb to the temptations. These addictions eventually become a part of their personality. Small habits like shopping compulsively or crossing the credit card limits are signals to take a serious note of our choices.

How we react to and approach the temptation, determines the quality of our life. Handle these addictions with a determined choice. Next time you are tempted, focus on the parts that are being affected by the obsession. Feel your solar plexus, chest, and throat areas. Decide whether you are happy with those consequences. No temptation is stronger than you, yourself. Use your power to say a big NO. Repeat if necessary. Make a list of your temptations, no matter how embarrassing they are. This will make you aware of what and how much you need to change.

## Some More Useful Tips:

### Be aware of the consequences the choices create

If you know that your son prefers cricket and you enrol him for a football club, he will resist. Both of you will be miserable. You will be miserable because you have spent the money and feel it is wasted and he will grudge that he is not being given a choice. In such a case, it is evident right from the beginning that the choice is not going to be fruitful. So be aware. Keep aside your ego and stop holding grudges. Discuss with him, make a wise choice, and create a different experience for you and your son.

### Be aware of your attitude

Viktor E. Frankl, even when he knew he was likely to die at the hands of the Nazis, said:

"We who lived in concentration camps can remember the men who walked through the huts comforting others, giving away their last piece of bread. They may have been few in number, but they offer sufficient proof that everything can be taken from a man but one thing: the last of the human freedoms—to choose one's attitude in any given set of circumstances, to choose one's own way."

(*Man's Search for Meaning* by Viktor E. Frankl)

There are different energies behind every act. When we choose, we are choosing an attitude, whether we are aware of it or not. Therefore, it is not important what we do. The most important thing is our attitude behind it. What is our attitude of gifting? Does giving gifts to friends make us a happy person? Do we give gifts as an investment or out of love? What is our attitude as a social worker? Is it a genuine desire to help people or do we want to gain popularity? Our attitude behind all our actions makes a difference on how we feel—happy or disappointed.

A lady complained that it was no use doing good to other people. All her life she claimed to have served her family and others. "But no one really cares," she moaned. She grudged everything and everybody. Further investigations revealed the glaring fault in her attitude. All her giving was merely an investment for her own personal ends. Extremely possessive and dominating by nature, she wished to win over others in exchange for the grand charities. When she faced resistance, she blamed others of ingratitude. All the giving is nullified by the attitude of taking that accompanies it. In social circles, receiving usually pressurizes us with the undercurrents of expectation it carries. A true giver is one whose motive is to benefit others. Such a person truly enjoys the sense of supreme happiness and satisfaction that springs from his action. But if there is a price tag attached to your giving, it will not yield any joy. And this knowledge will add to your power as a creator. Give as Nature gives. Nature is a silent giver and expects nothing in return. The purer the giving, the purer the happiness it begets.

> Small habits like shopping compulsively or crossing the credit card limits are signals to take a serious note of our choices.

It is never too late to change. We can't go back and undo what we did in the past, but we can do things differently from now onwards. It is time to quit digging. Put the shovel down, and start climbing out of the hole you've dug yourself into! No matter how old you are, you can start right now. Experiment with choices. If one choice does not work, try out something else. Arnold H. Glasgow wrote, "Ideas not coupled with action never become bigger than the brain cells they occupied."

Go from the simple to the complex. Start with small things like how much time you are spending on watching TV, studying, or playing. How you are using your money; what you are eating; how you sit, stand, or walk. Choose to smile today, come what may! Be in charge of every moment of your life. See what happens.

"Some part of getting a second chance is taking
responsibility for the mess you made in the first place."
(Jack Bauer, *24*, American T.V. Series)

# Take Responsibility for Your Life

There was some important work that had to be done, and Everybody was sure that Somebody would do it. Anybody could have done it, but Nobody did it. Somebody got angry because of this, since it was Everybody's job. Everybody thought Anybody could do it, but Nobody understood that Everybody wouldn't do it. It ended with Everybody blaming Somebody as Nobody did what Anybody could have done.

This is the general outlook we have towards life. Everybody feels the problem lies with the other. Everybody expects the other person to understand. Nobody looks inward at himself. Shel Silverstein has also reflected and emphasized this truth in this poem, apparently written for kids.

"Nobody loves me, nobody cares,

Nobody picks me peaches and pears.

Nobody offers me candy and Cokes,

Nobody listens and laughs at my jokes.

Nobody helps when I get into a fight,

Nobody does all my homework at night.

Nobody misses me, nobody cries,

Nobody thinks I'm a wonderful guy.

So, if you ask me who's my best friend, in a whiz,

I'll stand up and tell you NOBODY is!

But yesterday night I got quite a scare,

I woke up and Nobody just WASN'T there!

I called out and reached for Nobody's hand,

In the darkness where Nobody usually stands.

Then I poked through the house, in each cranny and nook,

But I found SOMEBODY each place that I looked.

I searched till I was tired, and now with the dawn,

There is no doubt about it—

NOBODY'S GONE!"

Many a times, this nobody appears in the form of various excuses and reasons we put forth, for not having achieved what we wanted, or what we deserved. Some of the following statements could be true for many of us.

- I dropped out of school because my parents were poor and from the wrong part of town.
- I wasn't promoted because I did not bribe him.
- I could not do it because . . .
- I could not get it because . . .
- It is not possible for me because . . .
- . . . is not . . . because . . .

People with this kind of attitude believe they are just unlucky; they think they are always right and their actions are always justified; they feel helpless and the victims of circumstances. Whereas, the root of their goof-ups could be traced back to their bad decisions or having lacked the courage to take some decisions, consciously or subconsciously, at some point of their lives in the past.

Children sneak their boogies on their parents' shoulders and sleeves when they are small or get their parents to wipe their nose. Over a period of time, they learn to do it themselves in a right way. But there are some who even after having grown into adults expect their parents to wipe their nose. They always expect things to be done for them by somebody else. It could be by the boss in the office or the spouse at home. They want people, circumstances, luck, and fate to take responsibility for their failures and unhappiness.

Then there are parents who always take their child's side. They refuse to accept that their child could do anything wrong. The message conveyed to the children is that they could get away with anything and everything just by denying responsibility for their actions. The result: their children become incapable of thinking objectively and adopt a shortcut method of always running away from the truth.

The consequences for not owning responsibility are not very pleasant ones. Such people are full of negativity with its various manifestations—hopelessness, anger, depression, and sadness—because they are not ready to take responsibility for their actions. The false self makes them critical of others. They lose their sense of seeing things objectively. Their expectations from others are high and they become more demanding. It comes in the way of their building good relationship with others, causing a lot of pain to others and themselves as well. The world is full of such 'poor souls' spreading unhappiness wherever they are and wherever they go.

It is true that society has a major hand in influencing our habits and beliefs. But as adults, we have the choice and capacity to change. When we tell others how they should make adjustments so that we can be happy, we are shirking from owning up and taking responsibility. This diverts our focus from the actions we ourselves could take to rectify the situation.

Do you have a strong view of the way things should be or the way people should behave? Do you hold other people responsible when something doesn't fit that view? It is time to work through it soon.

> The situation is not because of the wrong job, parents, environment, or any other person but us.

## Accept Responsibility

"Ninety-nine per cent of all failures come from people who have a habit of making excuses," said the great American scientist, George Washington Carver.

If you are one of those, it is time to change the course of your life by accepting responsibility for whatever good or bad happens in your life.

One of our friend's daughter's marriage was going through a rough patch. She genuinely wanted to save her marriage. During one of the counselling sessions with her, I tried to get her attention to some of the areas where she seemed to be contributing to the problem. She was highly offensive and agitated. Forget about owning, she even refused to give it a thought. The divorce was inevitable. What a heavy price to pay! Had she been a little honest to herself, the story would have been different.

We need to view ourselves as the cause and not as the effect. When we are the cause, we are giving ourselves a chance to act on our mistakes and change the outcome. If something does not turn up as planned, ask yourself, "What did I do or not do to create this? What do I need to do differently the next time, to get the desired results?" If we understand the relationship between cause and effect, we can control the outcome by changing the cause or our response to the cause.

We need to recognize the change in the present for us to change. If relationships are going haywire, examine yourself and see where you have gone wrong. The situation is not because of the wrong job, parents, environment, or any other person but you. Approach the problem with an open mind and positive outlook, for a change. You are bound to get a solution. Dietrich Bonhoeffer once wrote, "Action springs not from thought, but from a readiness for responsibility."

We need to make a personal inventory of all emotions. Make a diary if required.

As adults, we have choices that we can exercise. We can look within and find out how we are contributing to the problem. When we do that, apologies come naturally to us. Acknowledge, accept, and embrace it. Every time we accept our mistake, we are taking a step forward. We become aware of our blind spots. We can deal with the issues with ease. We are geared to change and ready to explore a new world and release the creativity in us. And there is a welcome change in our lives.

Remember, people who we resent may have done their best to their knowledge and awareness. We need to do the best to our knowledge and awareness.

## Stop being grouchy!

A squeaky wheel does get the grease first, but if you come off like a whacko, you're going to diminish your chances of getting what you want. Complaining is the negation of happiness. It is impossible to complain and be happy at the same time. Complaining is worse than doing nothing, for it is digging the groove one is in, deeper and deeper. Each time one complains, it becomes increasingly difficult to climb out of the ditch one has created for oneself.

Have you ever realized that people do not complain about things they cannot do anything about? For example, if it were not for gravity, we wouldn't fall down the stairs and break our bones or we wouldn't break any dishes. But when any of these things happen, we blame ourselves for our carelessness. We do not curse gravity. Not only that! We have rather found out different ways to use gravity to our advantage. We use drains to take away our waste. We ski, sky-dive, high jump—all of which require gravity. The reason is simple. We know that no amount of complaining will ever change the theory of gravity. So we have accepted it.

The circumstances we complain about are, by their very nature, situations we can change, but have chosen not to change. It is because making a change might take effort, money, and time on our part. It might be uncomfortable and difficult. We are not willing to take the risk of creating. We run the risk of failure, confrontation, being wronged or ridiculed. So we almost always end up complaining. We go to work and complain about our spouse; we come home and complain about our boss or the people at work.

Come out of your comfort zone. Instead of complaining to the wrong person, make a request to the person towards whom it is directed. Work out the strained relationships with spouses and parents. If a certain response is not getting the desired result, change the responses. The world doesn't owe us anything. We have to create it.

## Use 'I' statements, instead of 'You' statements

Generally, when we hear something hurtful, we express our hurt from 'you' point of view. For example: when the husband leaves the wet towel on the bed, the general reaction that comes from wife is, "You know how you drive me mad by always leaving the wet towel on the bed?" The better way to express our anger is "I feel irritated when I find the wet towel on the bed." Similarly, rather than saying, "You think I am dumb! I think you are both dumb and deaf," say, "I feel hurt when I am called dumb."

This way we are just expressing how we feel and think. We are taking responsibility for our own words, thoughts, and feelings. We are not passing judgment on the other person. To begin with, we can use the word 'I' instead of 'You' in our daily conversations. This way we are making the other person more receptive to our problem. It further leads to effective communication. 'I' statements help us to be more self-aware of our thoughts, words, and actions, which in turn brings clarity of mind. Though old habits die hard, but with efforts and practice, they do die.

> Each time one complains, it becomes increasingly difficult to climb out of the ditch one has created for oneself.

## Some valuable tips:

* Generally, the word 'responsibility' feels like a load on our shoulders because as children, we were always told, "Be responsible . . . Do this," "Behave responsibly . . . Do that," "When will you be responsible?" We feel we are being exploited in the name of responsibility. So we have developed a negative attitude towards the word 'responsibility.'

  Let's look at the word differently. Responsibility means 'the ability to respond' in a given situation. Sounds better? It does. Moreover, we feel empowered. When we respond to the best of our ability, we are benefited. We find a tremendous improvement in our relationships and life. And taking responsibility does not necessarily mean that it's your fault always. May be a less deserving candidate takes away your well-deserved promotion just because he is a relative of your boss. It's not really your fault! Taking responsibility means acknowledging your mistakes and responding appropriately to the situation.

- Look out for signals—your gut feeling, instinct, or inner voice always tells you something. Do not ignore this warning. These are meant to prevent any imminent danger. Pay attention to those late comings with alcohol on the breath. Did any friend warn you? Make enquires about it.

- Watch out the results you are producing. Is there something wrong in the outcome of any event or experience? It is time to change the responses. It could be spending money thoughtlessly, not eating right, meeting the wrong person . . . just about anything. Find out where you are making a mistake. Rectify it.

- Take a note of the conversations you have in your daily life. Listen to yourself. Is there a blaming pattern? Do you hear yourself holding your co-workers responsible for the unfulfilled targets? Are you cursing your luck for not being able to get through the examination? If yes, you are certainly into blame game.

- Take other people's feedback seriously. Remember, "If one person tells you you're a horse, they are crazy. If three people tell you you're a horse, there's conspiracy afoot. If ten people tell you you're a horse, it's time to buy a saddle." (Jack Rosenblum)

- Take responsibility on yourself. And if the situation demands, take responsibility of others' mistakes too. That is a super feat. That's what Lal Bhadur Shastri did. He resigned as the railway minister when two trains collided and resulted in many injuries. How many ministers show this kind of courage?

> 'I' statements help us to be more self-aware of our thoughts, words, and actions which in turn brings clarity of mind.

Though it seems scary to hold oneself accountable for the goof-ups in one's own life, but to see our dreams come true, it's not a bad bargain. Also, remember what a wise man once said, 'You can either be part of your plan or you will be part of someone else's plan.' The choice is yours.

# PART THREE

# What Are You Struggling With?

Each person is unique in temperament and personality. We and only we know what our deepest desires and struggles are! Once we find out the troublesome areas of our lives, we can get onto the job. For instance, if one is constantly faced with difficulties in marriage, then one needs to understand more about building relationships and work on it. If one is fighting with his uncontrollable anger, he needs to work more in this direction.

So instead of asking yourself what makes you happy, better ask yourself, 'what am I struggling with—family, friends, spouse, money, or what is it?' Reflect on things that make you struggle. Work on them by understanding the inner world. Result? End of struggle followed by happiness.

As far as I understand, there are three important issues most of us are struggling with:

> "Marriages are made in heaven,
> but are made to work here on earth."
>
> (Anonymous)

## The Miseries of Matrimony

### Marriage or a laughing stock!

Awoman awoke during the night to find that her husband was not in bed. She put on her robe and went downstairs. He was sitting at the kitchen table with a cup of coffee in front of him. He appeared to be in deep thought, just staring at the wall. She saw him wipe a tear from his eye and take a sip of coffee. "What's the matter, dear? Why are you down here at this time of night?" she asked. "Do you remember, twenty years ago when we were dating and you were only sixteen?" he asked. "Yes, I do," she replied. "Do you remember when your father shoved that shotgun in my face and said, "Either you marry my daughter or spend twenty years in jail?" "Yes, I do," she said.

He wiped another tear from his cheek and said, "You know . . . I would have been out today."

Jokes on marriage are endless, so are the miseries of wedlock. Michel De Montaigne once said, "Marriage is like a cage; one sees the birds from outside desperate to get in, and those inside equally desperate to get out." Marriage has become a laughing stock! There was a time when these kinds of jokes used to lighten and brighten up the mood of a person. But now they fail to create that effect. It's not funny anymore. The speed at which most marriages are falling apart is not really amusing.

The divorce rates are on the rise. Almost eighty per cent of the marriages experience adultery. Live-in relationships are getting more popular amongst the new generation. It seems like the sanctity of marriage has lost its charm at the altar of modern society. Should we blame it on daily soaps, or are the relationships just cracking? Every married couple seems to be pondering over this question. Sustaining a relationship in marriage has become a serious matter.

Well, there is succour for all those who feel trapped in the cage of marriage. We need to get to the root of the problem first.

> When we care more about our marriage than our marriage partner, we have misplaced the emphasis of our relationship.

## Welcome to the real world!

A man walking along a beach was deep in prayer. Suddenly the sky clouded and in a booming voice the Lord said, "Because you have tried being faithful to me in all ways, I will grant you one wish." The man said, "Build a bridge to Hawaii so I can drive over anytime I want." The Lord said, "Your request is very materialistic. Think of the enormous challenges for that kind of undertaking. The supports required to reach the bottom of the Pacific! Think about all the concrete and steel it would take! It will nearly exhaust several natural resources. I can do it, but it is hard for me to justify your desire for worldly things. Take a little more time and think of something that would honour and glorify me."

The man thought about it for a long time. Finally he said, "Lord, I wish that I could understand my wife. I want to know how she feels inside, what she's thinking when she gives me the silent treatment, why she cries, what she means when she says nothing's wrong, and how I can make a woman truly happy." The Lord replied, "Do you want two lanes or four lanes on that bridge?"

Even God does not have an answer when it comes to understanding a woman! A genius like Socrates could never understand what his wife meant when she said what she said. What to speak of an ordinary man!

And what did God say after he created man?

I could do better.

Almost every woman will vouch for this statement. Ask any woman what she thinks of a man. "A man is one of the most selfish and insensitive creations of God," pat comes the reply. And the blame game continues. Is it fair to fix blame on one gender? No. It takes two to make a successful marriage, and two for unsuccessful ones.

An institution is only as great as the relationship that makes up that institution. A great marriage is great because the couple has a great relationship and nothing less. Being married does not create a great relationship. But having a great relationship creates a great marriage. When we care more about our marriage than our marriage partner, we have misplaced the emphasis of our relationship. A happy relationship is one in which both enliven each other and add meaning to life.

Now the question is, 'Why is it so difficult for a man and a woman to understand each other?'

While our films fill us with immortal romance, the reality is totally different. We all expect to get married to a complete personality. Well, there is no harm in expecting it all, but the trouble starts when the expectations fall short or do not even move on the parameter graph. Most of the girls look for a guy who will be like her daddy, who is supposedly a caring, loving, understanding, and a humorous man. So somewhere deep down in her subconscious, the girl wants her husband to be successful and socially secured like her dad. A boy who thinks that his mother is the coolest woman on earth, cooks better than anyone else, handles the family, loves unconditionally, and caters to all his whims, is somewhere looking for the same qualities in a woman he'd like to marry.

A woman marries a man expecting he will change, but he doesn't. A man marries a woman expecting that she won't change and she does. The man understands slowly and painfully that his wife cannot match his mother and the wife slowly and quite painfully understands that nobody is as loving and intelligent as her father. Once the mating process is over, the real world comes to play. The guy snoring next to us becomes a stranger and the girl shouting at the top of her lungs is not the woman he married.

Psychologically, what we lack in ourselves is felt greater in this state. The false ego, mind, and set beliefs imprison us and the fear of losing our love remains on top of our mind. The person develops uncanny feeling of insecurity and unhappiness. Philosophically, true love is never conflicting. Each one of us has fought with our parents and siblings many times. These fights could have been the nastiest ones. But we always 'understand' the reasons and forgive them.

In case of a marriage, it is not love but a strong ego requirement that our spouse needs. When a spouse behaves in a way that fails to satisfy our ego, the feelings of fear, pain, anger, resentment, or jealousy start to crop up. Just like a drug fails to give a high after prolonged use, the same is the case in a relationship. After repeated denials and longings, it fails to give any pleasure. We become hurt and depressed.

Successful marriages are those which are handled well. We can always rectify our mistakes. Definitely not by divorcing but by working on it. Think of the time when your relationship was so meaningful! Think over the reason why a spouse who always waited for you at the bus stop, cannot tolerate if the table is laid two minutes late. What is stressing him out? What has turned your better half from a loving wife to a nasty woman? Love does not fly off in an instant. The process builds up slowly. If we fail to pick up clues, the time will come when it will explode in our face. It's important to understand the signals and address the problems before they consume us. It needs to be kept alive with humour and common sense. It requires a lot of tolerance and dedication on the part of both the partners for it to work.

There are no role models, as no two marriages are alike. When two people are no longer getting along and the hours of silence between them are increasing, one of them will have to step down to save the relationship from becoming a history. We have got to understand some of the basics of a relationship.

## Give space, more space

Personal space is as important to a healthy marriage as spending time together. Generally, it is the man who needs it more than a woman. Being nosy and taking account of each and every moment of your spouse can be irritating and exhausting. Enjoy your own space and let your spouse enjoy it too. If your spouse does not enjoy shopping, do not force him to go with you. Try going out with your friends instead. He will be grateful and you will be happy. Do not suffocate each other by breathing on each other's neck twenty-four hours a day. Respect each other's space and privacy. It is out of solitude that love gets fresh energy. If the other person does not realize, ask for it. Be specific about what kind of space you need—quiet, fun, holiday, sport . . . At the same time, be realistic about your expectations. Do not look for perfection in your partner. No man is perfect. No woman is perfect either. You yourself are not perfect.

Kahlil Gibran wrote it beautifully:

"You were born together, and together you shall be for evermore.

You shall be together when the white wings of death scatter your days.

Aye, you shall be together even in the silent memory of God.

But let there be spaces in your togetherness,

And let the winds of the heavens dance between you.

Love one another, but make not a bond of love:

Let it rather be a moving sea between the shores of your souls.

Fill each other's cup but drink not from one cup.

Give one another of your bread but eat not from the same loaf.

Sing and dance together and be joyous, but let each one of you be alone,

Even as the strings of a lute are alone though they quiver with the same music.

Give your hearts, but not into each other's keeping.

For only the hand of life can contain your hearts.

And stand together, yet not too near together:

For the pillars of the temple stand apart,

And the oak tree and the cypress grow not in each other's shadow."

> Respect each other's space and privacy.
> It is out of solitude that love gets
> fresh energy.

We need to treat each other as different entities, who prior to coming into each other's lives, have had different sets of concepts and different reasons and purposes to exist. None of us are born to fulfil another person's dreams. There is more to life than just being a spouse. We are the masters of our own love, and can give or take as much as we want to. This perspective will help us to understand, acknowledge, accept and respect our partner for what he is.

## Do not try to control the other person

Do not be livid that you cannot change others according to your wish, for there are so many things that you have not been able to change about yourself. We face disappointments when we try to control the other person. Controlling someone means stifling his individuality and creativity. It would be better if we keep this job to pest and traffic control people only. We should look at the positive side of considering ourselves complete with what our partner has and which we lack, rather than looking at our differences as negative. We should rejoice in each other's strength rather than indulging in our weaknesses.

There is no doubt that sometimes some kind of behaviour in our partner is unacceptable and we want them to change. If we begin with acceptance, we increase our chances of getting the desired results. It is a matter of showing and practicing some patience and we will find that our partner cannot remain immune to this thoughtfulness of ours for a long time. One of my friends fell in love with her husband because he was very neat and tidy. Well, the problem started when he started cleaning her cupboard too. He was a stickler for punctuality and she was always late. Well, something which started as an irritation, developed into amusement and ultimately into acceptance. She is getting to understand his method of madness and he is adjusting to hers. They are happy at the moment. Once you accept the person for what he is, things become easy and simple. But some people love playing mind games and bring discord in their lives. Remember, if this is the case, no one wins.

## Build up trust

Trusting one another means a solid relationship. Building up trust in a relationship requires a lot of effort and even more dedication. In fact, it takes a very high amount of regard for our spouse. We tend to do insensitive things, only when we have no regard for our partners. A man who spends money drinking beer in the pub every night, but fails to meet the basic requirements of the family, is simply selfish. Why would a woman spend more money than required on shopping when she knows that the money could have been used for something which both of them had been wanting for a long time? Why would a man cheat on his wife if he respects his wife? Being mean is not just bad but it also shows the amount of respect we have for our spouse. And remember, trust is built over a period of time. False promises and lies, however small they are, prove to be devastating in any relationship. Making and keeping promises consistently, goes a long way to build trust. There is no shortcut method.

> Do not be livid that you cannot change others according to your wish, for there are so many things that you have not been able to change about yourself.

## Build communication

Are you communicating with your spouse mainly through e-mails or messages? Then your relationship is red in tooth and claw. Do something about it right now. Today the world has become a global village. It does not take long to get to the other person in any part of the world. Then why has it become so difficult for husbands and wives, parents and children to have direct communication? Why is the gap gnawing? Why don't we have time to listen to one another anymore? Why are some people taking to sex and drugs instead of seeking companions? Why are couples living in huge houses with separate bedrooms? From whispering sweet nothings on long-distant calls, we are shouting at each other inside the four walls of our bedroom. Instead of bridging the gaps, we are building walls.

Fill in the communication gap and bring back laughter in your lives. Get to know your better half better. Pay attention to your partner's smallest needs. See what makes your spouse happy. Enlist for some courses together. Bring back the romance with those dates. Go for walks hand in hand. Rekindling the fire will make you happy and connect to each other.

Sometimes the fear of communication has its ramifications. Do not withdraw into a shell. Talk it out. Be fair. Make your communication clear, direct, open, and honest. Effective communication is essential in day-to-day life and especially in each relationship.

## Tips for good communication:

- The worst thing that one can do is to revel in other's misery. I once sniggered when my husband broke an expensive crystal brought from Muscat. He wasn't amused. But he did smile when the maid poured water over my painting that took me six days to complete. Moral of the story: Find something good to feel happy with each other.

- Enjoy every little event. Even if it means using each other's things by mistake and then laughing over it. Happiness is not programme bound.

- Do not dictate terms. No fascist ever won over people.

- Express yourself clearly and honestly. Don't beat around the bush. It could be frustrating.

- Whenever you feel cheated say, 'I feel cheated,' instead of saying, 'You cheated me!'

- Try to respond instead of reacting. You have a mind of your own. Be reasonable before retaliating. When you think and talk, chances are that going to the battlefield will not be necessary.

## How would I know unless you tell me?

Unless you are married to a psychic mind reader, your partner will not know what you want unless you ask him or her. It does not mean that your partner does not love you. It just means that he doesn't have psychic powers to understand what you want. I remember an article in *Reader's Digest* some twenty years back that read 'How do I know unless you tell?' It had an everlasting impression on my mind. It is true and really possible that someone could love you and not know what you want. The two don't necessarily go together.

To have your spouse know your expectations can save a lot of confusion. Be specific in asking. This also includes asking for hugs, asking for tenderness and intimacy, asking for acknowledgment and appreciation. Sure it is the coolest thing to do. Sometimes you do need to do such crazy things to win back your love. There comes a moment in everybody's life when one feels a little low for some reason or the other. Ask for compliments in plain simple words. I was amused and impressed when one of my friends told me the secret of how she dealt with her problem of feeling low at times. She would ask her husband to throw some words of praise in her honour as she needed a dose of morale booster. He would then oblige her by starting off with something like, "What wonderful hair you have! Wow . . . amazing!" She would start beaming, "Really! Tell me more." He would carry on, "The way you ironed my shirt today, I tell you, I have never seen such expertise. How do you manage to be good at everything?" They would burst out laughing and give each other a high five. Strangely enough, these seemingly childish acts brought both of them a lot of joy and a good laugh!

It is important to ask for feedback on the quality of life you are living (it sounds like a market survey—but do it. Try out this recipe sometimes. You will be surprised with the results. Ask for clarifications, if need be, to remove doubts. No partner can fulfil all your needs. Accept this or try fending for yourself.

> Sometimes the fear of communication has its ramifications. Do not withdraw into a shell. Talk it out.

## Avoid using absolute statements

A poor Chinese farmer found a beautiful black horse on his farm. The farmer and his only son were excited to see such a beautiful horse. The King of that place learnt about this wonderful horse and offered a huge sum to buy the horse. The farmer humbly rejected the offer. All the villagers told the farmer that he was stupid in rejecting the offer from the King. The farmer answered, "May be."

After a few days the horse was missing. The villagers once again told the farmer, "Do you realize you were unwise?" The farmer answered again, "May be." After a few more days, the horse returned with twenty other horses. The villagers now told the farmer, "You were really wise by not selling the horse." The farmer again answered, "May be."

The farmer's only son while training the horses fell down and broke his leg. Meanwhile, a war broke out in China, and all youngsters had to go to war except the farmer's son, as he was not fit. The villagers once again said, "You are lucky, your only son is saved." The farmer yet again said "May be." (*Looking at Life Differently* by Swami Sukhabodhananda)

The insight we get from this story is that things are relative. When you make an absolute statement, you are being judgmental. You leave no scope for flexibility or change. When you form an opinion about someone, do not give absolute statements such as: You are a cheat; He is cranky; She is a gone case . . . This way you leave communications open.

During one of my counselling sessions, when the marriage of my client was going through a rough patch, I observed that most of the time she was using absolute statements in her interaction with her spouse. I pointed this out to her. This realization changed her entire equation with her husband.

Avoid using words such as always, every day, all the time. These words offend a person. And how can you be sure about a person in absolute terms? Replace these words with sometimes, at times, most of the times . . . Now see the difference between the two statements, "You are always late." and "I have noticed that sometimes you are late." The reaction to these two statements will be totally different.

May be nobody ever drew your attention to such small things so far. It is never too late. Growing up in a relationship is like learning to drive a car smoothly. We get to have a few dents and a few bumps before we have the flair for driving it. We can't take it off straight away. We have to be patient and willing to give it a serious and sincere try, not taking things for granted. Once the dynamics of relationships have been understood, we will have fewer potholes and more bridges. I am sure it is worth making this small effort to save something as important as marriage and turn it into a healthy, happy, and rejuvenating one.

> "Before I got married, I had six theories about bringing up children; now I have six children and no theories."
>
> (John Wilmot, Earl of Rochester)

# Parenting – The Most Difficult 'Job' in Today's Modern World

There is no career more important than parenting. It begins from the day the child is born. It is easy to become a parent but not so easy to bring up the child right. It is much more than just meeting their materialistic requirements. Future of the children and the nation depends on how well the parents do their job. Raising a child is the most demanding job especially so in today's complex world where parents themselves are contending with their careers and staggering marriages. A child goes through different developmental stages. Each level brings a new challenge and requires different skills on the part of the parents. From changing diapers and spending sleepless nights by the side of the baby to child parenting, right through teenage, parenting is one tough job for any parent. They have tremendous power and huge responsibility as parents. Being good parents means creating a loving and safe environment for children to help them grow into happy and healthy adults—both physically and mentally. The important thing to understand is—which phase the child is going through and how to handle it. Parents' parenting styles must evolve as the child grows if they want to stand out from rest of the crowd as successful parents.

Good self-esteem is a major key to a happy and healthy life. To me, if parents can build good self-esteem in their children and are capable enough to help them sail through their teenage period with love and understanding, they have done a good job. Here is some user-friendly information for parents on how to raise their child's self-esteem and inculcate in them certain skills that will help them cope with the stress that comes with teenage.

*"How you treat your child, he will treat himself.
And how he treats himself, he will treat the world."*
(Anonymous)

# Self-Esteem and Children

Cho Seung-Hui, 23, a South Korean senior in the University of Blacksburg hit the headlines when he carried out America's deadliest carnage, gunning down thirty-three students and teachers before shooting himself. In a vitriolic note he railed against 'rich kids' and stated, "You caused me to do this." Though it is one of the extreme examples of how a feeling of low self-esteem can lead a person to discontentment and destruction, yet it is clear how dangerous the consequences of low self-esteem can be.

Self-esteem is our overall opinion of how we honestly feel about and value ourselves. Self-esteem involves judging our worth as a person. It ranges from too positive to too negative. Neither extreme is healthy. People who have an unrealistic view of themselves are boastful and arrogant. People with low self-esteem think themselves as worthless. Healthy self-esteem lies in the middle of the two. It makes a person feel confident and have a positive view of one's strengths, abilities, and accomplishments. He knows his basic worth but does not feel the need to compare it with others. On the other hand, people with low self-esteem put little value on their own opinions and ideas. They think that they aren't 'good enough.' Low self-esteem is like a heavy sack on the back. When we try to climb the stairs of life with this load, we stagger at every step, and ultimately tumble down.

The feeling of worthlessness is particularly prevalent in today's adolescents. The vast majority of children between the age group of twelve to twenty are bitterly disappointed with who they are and what they represent. The high incidents of crimes and suicides relate largely to a lack of self-esteem. It is a sad and serious situation. Self-worth is not only the concern of those who lack it; the health of entire society depends on it. Widespread mental illness, neuroticism, hatred, alcoholism, drug abuse, violence, and social disorder are likely to occur in its absence. When we are not paying attention to this vital personality meter, we never know how and when bottled-up feelings take a dangerous form.

Charity begins at home and so does self-esteem. "I'd build self-esteem first, and the house later." This quote by Diane Loomans in his book *If I Had My Child to Raise over Again*, speaks volume of the importance of self-esteem. As parents, take care of what affects the child at various stages of life, before he takes on to the world.

Help your child build self-worth.

## Study behavioural patterns

It is normal for children to go through times when they feel low. We all feel less confident in certain areas and think negatively of our accomplishments or physical appearance. However, when we feel bad about ourselves in too many areas of life and these feelings become long-standing, they can damage our self-esteem. Low self-esteem can appear in the way we look, behave, and interact with others. Cho Seung Hui was a silent loner who never made eye contact. He was jealous, envious, and uncommunicative. He was a fan of violent video games and was a sexually frustrated young man. He had all the symptoms of low self-esteem. Wise parents

162

will watch out for the symptoms and take action before it gets too late.

> Low self-esteem is like a heavy sack on the back. When we try to climb the stairs of life with this load, we stagger at every step, and ultimately tumble down.

## Consider these points:

- Children with positive feelings about themselves perform better in school than children with low self-esteem.

- Children who feel good have positive relationships with others unlike children who don't like themselves.

- Children with low self-esteem are less creative than children with a healthy self-esteem.

- Kids with low self-esteem nurture self-critical thoughts like, 'I'm no good' or 'I can't do anything right.' They have a tough time finding solutions to problems which in turn make them passive, withdrawn, or depressed.

- Does your child laugh at everything or constantly indulges in childish pranks to draw attention? It is time to pay attention.

- Depression in teenage is the result of a poor self-image. It often leads to suicide. When a child has a low opinion of himself, he has the tendency to underestimate his chances in life. Be alert to this symptom in your child.

- When a girl dresses provocatively, chances are that she is being neglected in the house and is trying to seek attention from outside. She is likely to become an easy prey to any guy who shows interest in her.

## Who puts the price tag?

The price tag attached to a child is his self-esteem. All relationships close to him like parents, siblings, peers, teachers, and other important adults are powerful; though it is the parents who, in most occasions, put the price tag. Children learn their first lesson about self-esteem from their parents. Even a two-year-old child can sense whether he is loved or not. He asks himself, "Who loves me and needs me? Who loves me the most?" All unspoken thoughts get embedded in the subconscious mind. Many beliefs we hold about ourselves today, reflect messages we have received from such people over time. Most maladjusted youth or adults have had broken childhoods. If we have been receiving a positive feedback, we are more likely to see ourselves as worthwhile. However, negative feedback and criticism, ridicule or being devalued by others, often results in depression and a low self-worth.

Some other reasons a child may lose self-respect include being called by nicknames ridiculing their appearances, for example: pig, piddy, kallu; making faces when they make mistakes; refusing to touch, kiss, or play with them; interrupting every time they try to say something. But the most important factor that has the biggest impact on our self-esteem is our own thoughts. Thoughts include 'self-talk'—what we tell ourselves; our perception of situations; and our beliefs about self, other people, and events. For example, how we measure success and failure in life affects our sense of self-worth. A series of perceived successes can lead to feelings of positive self-worth and high self-esteem. In the same way, a series of perceived failures can make one feel low and inferior.

## How to increase self-worth in our child?

Raising children with good self-image is a very demanding job. It needs to be understood and fostered at the core level by parents.

Positive atmosphere allows him to grow with positive thoughts and negative environment with negative thoughts. Let's see how parents can make their children feel good about themselves.

## Love your children unconditionally

Love your children irrespective of how they perform academically or in sports. Children don't want expensive things but love. Give them a lot of hugs and pats on the back. Unconditional love from parents gives them strength to bounce back after failure or rejection and sail through the period of self-doubts which they face in plenty at this age.

Help your child start and end his day in a loving and optimistic way—not with a gruff. Waking up and sleeping should be a pleasurable experience like gently stroking the forehead or hugging and kissing good morning and good night. Treat him with respect. Give him space. Use 'please' and 'thank you' generously.

A child, who is loved, loves himself. Only a person who loves himself is happy being in his own company.

## Be positive

Children take parents' reaction to their failures far more seriously. Bitter and hurtful words may cause an irreparable damage to their trust in self.

Some parents tend to remind their children of their failure even after their children have got married and have school-going children. But some are wiser. When I was in school, my friend's brother failed for the first time and shocked everyone. Seeing the gloomy atmosphere prevailing, as though someone had died, my friend's father said to the boy, "Let's celebrate today, so that you don't fear failures in life as they are the stepping stones to success."

It lifted everyone's spirits. Today he is a successful man—both in personal and professional life.

Positive talks are magical. When we encourage children to be positive, they dare to take risks in life. Where there is negative talk, there is depression and anxiety; where there is positive talk, there is joy and happiness.

A positive child grows up to be a go-getter in adult life. Share his pains and joy. Rejoice in his small world. But first apply it on yourself.

> Help your child start and end his day in a loving and optimistic way—not with a gruff.

## Be generous with praise

Don't be a miser in praising the child when you see something good in him. Generally, we are on the look out to catch children falter and give them sermons. Try catching them doing good things too. Applaud the effort, even if the outcome is not so great. They need it most when they goof-up. They look forward to your trust and reassurance that they are capable children who you are proud of.

## Teach children to make choices and to take responsibility for them

Parents, who make choices on behalf of their children, make them dependent on others. Brainstorm the choices and their pros and cons together with the child. Help him with the alternatives and in evaluating results. Start with simple choices. We can begin with, "Will you do your homework now or after watching this cartoon programme?", "Will you eat boiled eggs or an omelette?"

## Teach your child to be brutally honest

A weak person cannot be honest. Honesty is the attribute of strong. An honest child is non-judgmental in his view of others. A child who likes himself does not feel threatened by others different from him. He accepts a person for who he is. He doesn't have to resort to cheap tactics of lying or demeaning others to feel better. He is not only receptive to everybody's ideas, but capable of forming his own opinion and taking his own wise decisions too. These are crucial things that add to his character-building and make him strong in later years. This eventually leads to a better self-esteem.

## Prepare your child to leave the nest

"Some parents could do more for their children by not doing so much for them." (Author unknown)

Dependency on parents for longer than required gives children a comfortable and happy adolescence but a painful adulthood. Dependent children are never confident of their capabilities. So it is a must for parents to start the process of making them independent as early as possible. In fact, the detaching process starts from the moment the umbilical cord of the newborn child is snipped off. Though we want to bind children forever, as wise parents we need to prepare ourselves and them for the inevitable. Children need to be taken out of their comfort zone slowly to face the harsh realities of life. Parents need to work themselves out of the job, so that when they are no more, children are capable enough to live a happy and fulfilled life. To raise independent, motivated kids, the process has to be started as early as the time of infancy.

Start gradually, one step at a time. Don't expect children to become independent instantly. Let the child make choices as early as five years of age. If you see the child struggling with simple tasks, let him learn on his own. Stop spoon-feeding him. Unless he comes and asks, do not push yourself to do it. This way the child learns to make opinions and use his mind. Let him understand, experience, and deal with the results. Sometimes, you might just have to look the other way if your child pairs mismatched clothing or picks shoes that don't look right. The key is that if the child is safe and comfortable, it is perfectly okay. Every child learns differently. Don't compare him to friends, cousins, neighbours, or strangers. He may develop complexes. Sometimes you need to give a kick to the child to close the door on him. If need be, don't hesitate.

> Dependency on parents for longer than required gives children a comfortable and happy adolescence but a painful adulthood.

## A Father's Role

Most children refer to their father as their role model. It says a lot about the influence a father has on his children. A stern dad may win obedience and a lenient one may gain vote, but both fail to make effective fathers. None of them wins respect or contributes towards well-adjusted kids. Anything done in extreme is bad. There has to be a combination of love, understanding, trust, and communication.

No doubt all parents love their children, but most Indian men fail to express affection. It has been drilled into their mind that a man is not manly if he exposes his feelings. This fear prevents dads to be open about their feelings of love for their children. Fortunate is the man who escapes this unfortunate early conditioning.

Why all this caution? Forget about what you have been taught. Become a person who can risk and tolerate more happiness and affection. Although, the fathers of the new generation are far more expressive, they still need to fine-tune their parenting skills to make children feel worthy. Establish new rules—your own model for what a man should be. Start by kissing and hugging. Limiting your honest feelings is not healthy. To begin with, 'Fake it, till you make it.'

Dr. Sheehan summarizes the concept of developing healthy self-esteem with the following encouragement: "Self-esteem should not be based on what we do, but rather, who we think we are. After all I am not what I do. I am the precious human being that does it. If I make a mistake I am not the mistake, but rather the awesome learning machine that is capable of correcting mistakes."—Michael R. Sheehan Ph.D., Self-Esteem, Inc.

Our children give us the opportunity to become the parents we always wished we had. Why not rectify the mistakes our parents made out of ignorance? Why not make them feel great about themselves and create a healthy, happy world!

"When I was a boy of fourteen, my father was so ignorant I could hardly stand to have the old man around. But when I got to be twenty-one, I was astonished by how much he'd learned in seven years."

(Mark Twain)

## Troublesome Teens

A wise old gentleman purchased a modest home near a junior high school after retirement. The first few weeks of his retirement passed off quietly. Then a new school year began.

The very next afternoon three young boys, full of after-school exuberance, came down his street, banging merrily on every trash can they encountered. The percussion continued day after day, until finally the wise old man decided to take some action.

The next afternoon, he walked out to meet the young percussionists as they banged their way down the street. Stopping them, he said, "You kids are a lot of fun. In fact, I used to do the same thing when I was your age. Will you do me a favour? I'll give you each a dollar if you promise to come around every day and do this."

The kids were elated and continued to do a bang-up job on the trash cans. After a few days, the old-timer greeted the kids again, but this time he had a sad smile on his face. "This recession's really putting a big dent in my income," he told them. "From now on, I'll only be able to pay you fifty cents to beat on the cans." The noisemakers were obviously displeased, but they did accept his offer and continued their afternoon ruckus. A few days later, the wily retiree approached them again as they drummed their way down the street.

"Look," he said, "I haven't received my Social Security cheque yet, so I won't be able to give you more than twenty-five cents. Will that be okay?" "A lousy quarter?" the drum leader exclaimed. "If you think, we're going to waste our time beating these cans around for a quarter, you're nuts!"

Smart guy!

What's your take on troublesome teens? Are you skilful enough to handle your teenage children? If not, then living with teens can be a harrowing experience as they have a special ability to drive their parents insane. They can be on your nerves nearly all day long. "My child has been so loving and obedient. I don't know what has gone wrong with him! He is not the same. He has become so difficult." I have heard these statements quite often during the counselling sessions. Parents of teenagers can't help wondering, "Is this the same baby I held in my arms sometime back?" We never know when children grow up! We could be in for a shock or surprise anytime of the day or night.

Teenagers can irritate parents till kingdom come! You feel mentally challenged. Your beliefs and curfew timings are questioned. Brace yourself to hear and answer 'Why' at least ten times a day. From being a doting dad, you become a pesky pa. If, as a dad, you have not yet taken a chill pill, this is the time you will need it most. Till the teen has entered the next phase of life, you are dealing with a rebel without a cause, pause, or whatever! The task becomes even more difficult with the new challenges each new generation comes with. But at the same time, every parent has the potential to improve and become a proud parent to their teenagers, only if they are willing to grow.

## Understand adolescent's irrational behaviour

Teenagers are neither kids nor adults. These in-between years can take a toll or become golden years of their lives, depending on how we handle them. As we cannot fix anything, unless we have an understanding of the components—be it a TV, computer, or mixer, we cannot handle teenagers if we do not have an understanding of the factors responsible for the irrational behaviour in them.

We grow and change throughout our lives. But the physical and psychological changes that take place in a child during early adolescence are especially evident. It is often a very turbulent time. We, as parents, need to be aware of these changes.

> Those who have not met with affection at home, fall for intimate experiences outside the house.

## An age of dramatic physical changes

A teenager goes through many bodily changes. If you, who has already gone through this phase of life, don't understand, how do you expect it from a child for whom it is the first time? Both boys and girls get too conscious of their physical appearances—something they had never bothered about before. Suddenly, they start looking more mature and big. Acne, pimples, and changing hormones create restlessness in them. Some teenagers are late bloomers. This puts them into awkward positions. They are teased about their sexual immaturity. Locker-room teasing can take a toll on them. They may start harbouring negative thoughts when they are teased. The teen wonders if he will ever be normal! They are confused and embarrassed. Self-esteem is at the lowest ebb. Usually, girls enter puberty two years earlier than boys of the same age. How parents, friends, and others react to them has a lot of impact on how they grow into adults. If their reactions are positive, they are likely to be more receptive and grow into mature adults. Or else, trouble lies ahead.

This is the time they need more sleep and better nutrition. Whatever the rate of growth, many young teens have an unrealistic view of themselves and need to be reassured that differences in growth rates are normal. A healthy parental guidance, constant encouragement, and assurance is required by children.

> With roots, give them wings too.

## Understand their emotional upheavals

Mood swings are common for most teens. They seem edgy all the time and may become overly sensitive and self-conscious. One can't predict when they will be happy or sad. Tempers may fly off anytime, almost anywhere. They may blow up on seeing a pimple on the face before a party. A girl may not want her mother to follow her to school or tuitions any more. The teen may reject your hand on the shoulder. They think you are not a parent but a push-over. Do not get upset. Do not resent, if you do not wish your child to clamp up. Carol Bleifield, a middle-school counsellor in Wisconsin, explains, "One minute, they want to be treated and taken care of like a small child; five minutes later they are pushing adults away, saying, "Let me do it." You may help them to understand that they are in the midst of some major changes."

Some mood swings can be excessive or dangerous. Keep an eye for them. Emotional disturbances can create chaotic situations. Be on the lookout for excessive emotional swings or long-lasting sadness in your child. These can suggest severe emotional problems. Try talking to his friends and find out what the matter is. Do not give up.

## Social changes

Are you getting irritated with the phone bills in the house? You are not the only parent who is! This is the stage when things all around excite teenagers. They start expanding their social circle. They want to find a career, social acceptance, and peer acceptance. Those who have not met with affection at home, fall for intimate experiences outside the house. Promiscuity in teens affects the mental psyche eventually. They look for approval, friendship, acceptance, and compassion all the time. If they develop an inferiority complex, they will look for appreciation elsewhere. Look for signals that suggest more than normal intimation. Chances of exploitation are tremendous at this stage. They tend to identify themselves with someone strong. If they do not have parents to come back to, they may turn wayward. Check out whom they idolize. If it is a regular sportsman or film star or rock star, it's okay. If the idol is some anti-establishment leader, or terrorist, or some skinhead, you better be warned.

As a parent, give the teen a healthy identity before someone else gives it to him. Change your attitude to bring back the teen into the fold. He will be appreciative of this later in life. To put them on the right track, introduce them to some healthy social group.

Society changes with every generation. Influences like movies, television, internet, video games, and competition are ruling this world. The challenge lies in compromising on some issues and adjusting to some. The 'No Negation' rules with teenagers should be used in extreme cases like drugs, drunken driving, pregnancy, or assault. If your teen is into violent video games, it is time to sneak into his friend circle and battle the negative influences. Try to seek some productive form of entertainment for the teen. At this stage, teens are looking for freedom of expression and independence. Let them see the world with their own eyes, not yours. With roots, give them wings too.

If we have an understanding of all this, we, as parents, can make a lot of difference to their growth and make them and ourselves really proud.

After having taken the first step towards effective parenting, let's see how we can transform these teen years into happy years for our children as well as for us.

## Are you handling teens with kid gloves?

Don't! And if you overreact with rage, then you will end up pulling your hair. Teenagers need to be treated a little differently. Parents and teens can live together, more or less harmoniously, only if parents know what to expect and what not to and are willing to make some adjustments themselves in the way they think and act. What we need is a preventive technique to have a trustworthy relationship with a teen in the house.

Here is a back-up kit combined with a first-aid kit to buck up our parenting skills.

## Keep strong family bonding

Parents are the most influential factor in children's life. A stable home means a rock solid relationship. If children are raised in a happy, healthy home, they can reap benefits for a lifetime. Conversely, it can cause them serious long term psychological and physical scars. A harmonious relationship between parents gives them a sense of security and they grow as confident and happy citizens.

Remember, teens don't like to come to an empty home. They need family, even though they may want privacy. If you both have late working hours, you need to make some adjustments to be available to your child. Know your priorities. Understand where to draw a line. Spend enough time at home with the family. The way you project yourself, affects the way your teenage child will project himself to the world.

> All children are 'Columbus' till a certain age.

**Someone put it very beautifully:**

- First be a person
- Then a partner
- Then a parent
- Then a professional

If you want to give your child a congenial environment to grow, take care of yourself first. Remember, a happy and a healthy mother makes a happy and healthy family. Keep yourself sound—both mentally and physically. Do not be at loggerheads with your spouse. It is not a pleasant sight for a teenager to witness his parents fighting. Some parents want to win the approval of the child at the cost of the other. They may become manipulative. It will percolate to their adult life and ruin their happiness. Let this not be the case with you. Discuss parenting and dealing with the teenager between yourself first and then go by the rules. Make sure you both are understanding and unanimous on decisions. Dealing with a teenager is either easy or difficult, depending on how you both choose to handle it.

## Building relationship with teenagers

We live in an age where we have forgotten what life is all about. We have e-mail, fax machines, and digital phones to stay connected with the world, yet we find it difficult and cannot take out time to stay connected with our own family. It is interesting to watch ladies discussing soap operas in parties. They keep themselves updated with what's happening in the on-screen life of actors, their children, grandchildren and even great grandchildren, but they are hardly aware of what is going on in the lives of their own children or spouse. They mostly react to the second-hand information about their own children, provided to them by somebody else. Of what good is it? Suddenly somebody informs or misinforms them and they blow everything out of proportion. We need to sort our lives by being our own writer, director, and actor.

Media exposure has widened the mind of today's children. Music channels, soap operas, beauty pageants, and films have a big impact on children today. But how many teens realize that this is a make-belief world? Having communication lines open is of vital importance. Talk rationally. Treat your teens with more respect. Don't jump to any conclusion if you see your daughter laughing with a male friend. She is innocent. Let her be, till you see something outrageous in her behaviour. Don't yell. Discuss. Only if a dialogue is not fruitful should you think of taking stern action. Controlling, especially at this age, never works. Remember, this is the time she also wants to explore the world—drugs, sex, boyfriends, and alternate relationships. Monitor subtly and handle tactfully. Do not get into a power struggle.

**Some communication tips for parents:**

We can hit an egg and open it or keep it warm and the egg will open itself naturally. We can yell, shout, punish, or develop a good warm relationship and get what we want effortlessly. The choice is ours.

- Privacy is not limited to adults. We need to respect teens' privacy too. Do not invade into their space. They are widening their horizons. Keep off! Trespassing is dangerous! Step in only when required.

- Be friends. Stop treating them like children. Remove the phrases 'I told you so,' 'Don't you dare' from your vocabulary. If your communication ends up with the same boring lecture, they will soon start avoiding you.

- Rather than imposing a curfew on their going out, tell them how to take care of themselves. This will teach them a few ideas about responsibility.

- If you have promised something, keep it up! If you keep to your side of the honour, they will too.

- Set an example yourself. Practice what you preach. Quoting others will not work. Be truthful, if you wish your child to be so. Apologize, if you make a mistake. Children are very observant. Do not make the mistake of underestimating them.

- Enjoy their growing-up period. Laugh at their jokes; enjoy their talks. Instead of being troublesome, let trendy teens perk you up. Have light conversations too.

- Stop nagging them. Be tactful if you want to stop them from doing something. The more you ask them not to do something; greater will be their desire to do the same.

A small boy saw a small girl carrying an apple.

He told the girl, "Would you like to play a game with me?"

The girl asked, "What game?"

He said, "Adam and Eve."

The girl said, "Good—what has to be done then?"

The boy said, "You tempt me, you say 'don't eat this apple' and I will eat it."

If Adam had not been told to not eat from the tree of knowledge, he would never have bothered about it. The very command created the temptation. Be tactful. Give the choices, not denials.

- Last, but not the least. Let your child be unique. All children are 'Columbus' till a certain age. What is taboo is desirable for their little existence. Let them explore while keeping an eye on them and guiding them gently with a little push in the direction we know is right. Remember, we know this right direction not because we were born with divine knowledge but because we were all 'Columbus' once. Let them pursue their ambitions. If a child is fond of doing event management, do not compel him to take up medicine. Let him discover his talents.

> Do not get into a power struggle.

## Listen with empathy

Empathic listening means listening with understanding. If you feel you are unable to understand a person because he is not ready to listen to you, you should have been listening to him, not talking. A doctor cannot prescribe till he diagnoses. Same way, you cannot understand before you patiently hear someone.

The right kind of listening is to get into the person's frame of mind and see things from his perspective as no two persons or problems are alike. When the person is sharing something personal with you, he just needs psychological support and wants to be accepted the way he is, in a non-judgmental way.

Here are some tips to develop better and effective listening skills:

- Stop what you are doing and give your full attention to the person you are listening to. I have heard about the nomadic Maasai herdsmen. When they have a get-together, they keep a talking stick. Whoever holds the stick is allowed to speak while others listen attentively. No one interrupts. Whoever wants to say something, has to wait till he is handed over that stick. There is a lot to learn from their custom.

- Give prompts—nodding, smiling, saying "mms."

- Let the child know you are always there to listen to him, whether it's about a falling out with a friend, a failure to make the football team, or disappointing marks in an exam. Stress, that making mistakes is not just about failure. It is an opportunity to learn how to get things right.

- Plan family meetings on a regular basis. It may be having dinner together or organizing picnics on weekends. They don't have to be long ones, just having them is enough. It gives everybody a chance to know what is going on in everybody's day-to-day life and things can be sorted out at the same time.

- Don't shout from a distance. Get up and go to the person who you want to talk to. Make sure your child makes eye contact while talking to you or somebody else. Not doing it is a sign of low self-esteem.

Invest in emotional banking with children. Believe me, it's the best long-term investment a parent can gift to a child. Enjoy watching your teenager blossom into a young adult. It will be as breathtaking as it was when you first held the newly born in your arms. Enjoy your parenthood! May no one ever have to ask, "Who has raised your children?"

*"To keep the heart unwrinkled, to be hopeful, kindly, cheerful, reverent—that is to triumph over old age."*
(Thomas Bailey Aldrich)

# In the Autumn of Your Life

Nirja Sharma, in her late eighties, was spending her days alone inside the four walls of her huge bungalow. She lost her husband during one of his morning walks in a hit-and-run case while crossing the road. They had two sons, both settled in the United States. They came for a few days for the funeral. Mentally, she had prepared herself to shift with them as she had no one to take care of her. But to her utter disappointment, they did not even ask her. May be they feared if they asked, she might agree. She spent the rest of her days alone, waiting for the phone to ring, to hear a voice other than her own. She hardly had any visitors. She had no one to talk to. Sometimes she would catch hold of the boy who used to deliver food at her place, as she was too old to cook, till one day, she was found murdered in the bedroom.

This is not a single case. In April 2008, an old lady named Karma Devi was found abandoned by her family outside a shopping complex in the JNU campus. She was so old that she could barely walk without support. She was left crying under a tree with a plastic bag containing a few clothes.

Though they are extreme cases, elderly abuse is certainly on the rise. The abandonment of parents by children is making waves. It's a pathetic sight to spot an old man looking for somebody to talk to or an old woman sitting in some corner of a park with a deserted look in her eyes.

The issue of old people's miseries is drawing intense public attention.

> With the advancement of science, life has been prolonged but so have the emotional miseries.

## 'I hope I die before I get old'

Indian family values are degenerating. Gone are the days when people were proud of entering the silver years of their lives. Old age used to signify wisdom. The youthful demeanour never left them. But in today's scenario, old age is a grim reminder of the happy youthful days. Old people feel neither happy nor safe. Times have changed and so has society's views on the elderly. The parents whose whole life revolved around their children, the parents who spent their life fulfilling the dreams of their children, are considered as burdens. They are categorized as old fashioned, outdated, and senile. Once they are past their best, they are disrespected and humiliated. Any kind of advice to them is treated as interference in their lives. Children of this generation are self-centred. They can spend hours gossiping with friends on mobiles or going out partying every day, but fail to update themselves on the affairs of their parents. They prefer to go on a holiday or watch TV instead of visiting parents on their birthdays or anniversaries. The old in the family are made to do errand jobs like getting vegetables from the market or babysitting their grandchildren without any appreciation.

Earlier, grandparents dreamt of having grandchildren in their arms and narrating fairy tales to them. But today's grandchildren are busy with video games and computer. Parents are even busier. The pride in today's youth for the wise elders is missing. This is a sad scenario for most seniors. Instead of looking at their well-spent years with happiness and satisfaction, they are bitter. They pass each day with trepidation. As a result, many old people suffer from psychosomatic disturbances and adjustment and behavioural problems. With the advancement of science, life has been prolonged but so have the emotional miseries. The blame for unhappy old age is blatantly put on children.

Now looking at this, approaching old age is frightful. No one wants to step into this phase of life willingly. "I hope I die before I get old," the opening line of Pete Townshed's song, seems to be every old man's desire.

## Other side of the story

Is it fair to hold children responsible for their parents' unhappy old age? Is it justified to label them as selfish? Aren't parents selfish too? I spoke to some of the younger generation children. Here is what most of them have to say:

The parents' decision to have children is not an altruistic act as they make it out to be. Be it to have a son as *budhape ka sahara* or to enjoy the feeling of parenthood, there is always an element of self-interest involved. Parents hope to re-live their dreams through their children. They are made to fight their parents' battle, not their own. They want everything to happen their way. A universal statement made by parents is "We sacrificed so much to give you a good life." Thanks. Sounds noble! But don't pass on your unfulfilled dreams to us in the name of sacrifices, as we, too, have our own dreams. At the end of the day, we want to get the satisfaction of having done what we wanted to do, not what others wanted from us. We don't want to be a part of this vicious circle of being frustrated parents and producing frustrated children. Better we live our dreams rather than asking our children to live them for us. Parents expect a gift in return of a gift. This is not correct. Let the gift given to the children be passed on to the next generation. Parents are the starting lines in our lives and they should stop at that, as they are not the finishing lines.

They expect to be looked after like children. They enjoy behaving like kids. Have you forgotten how irritating it used to be for you as parents when we, as teenagers, used to behave like one? Will a thirty-year-old look cute running after butterflies? The joke is about how you get into a reverse gear when you grow older; sounds cute and endearing only during dinner or coffee table conversations. But when some old people take this whole thing too literally, it is not really funny! Children are just a good pretext for their tensions and unhappiness. When not taken too kindly, the blame is conveniently palmed off on the younger generation.

Parents, in general, are irrationally temperamental. It becomes very confusing for children. They fail to cope with the stress that comes from the goal-oriented life and the same old expectations of the parents to be their Shravan Kumar. The values that children need to achieve the two different goals are totally contradictory. They fail to understand what makes a good son or a daughter or a unique individual—they are supposed to be. These are the views of the young generation on the issue of being irresponsible towards old parents. It is not only the adults but children are frustrated too. Both are facing problems that were not known before. In a way, both seem to be right.

I think parents have mentally conditioned their mind to think that they are incapable of taking care of themselves in old age. I know one such mother who ruined her son's life just to secure her old age.

Despite having cleared his MBA entrance exam, he was not allowed to take admission. He was rather forced to apply for a clerical job in the same small town where she lived—the place that had no future for him. Not only that; he was coaxed into marrying his elder brother's widow who had a teenage daughter from her previous marriage. The whole idea was to be looked after by children in the old age. But look at the dichotomy! Just a few months after his having taken up the job as a clerk, she died of a heart attack. Poor boy! He curses his mother for having smothered his life for her own selfish reasons. Had she allowed him to pursue his dreams, he would have been a happy soul today!

Ageing is a natural process. We need not react to old age as if something unknown and unexpected has taken place. There is no need to make such a big deal out of it. Old age is like any other stage in life. Any stage, that we haven't gone through yet, is challenging. Every phase has its own traumatic experiences and demands. Being a teenager is as hard or as nice as being old. Why don't we just dwell in the beauty of every stage including old age, unveiling slowly what it has to offer?

We need to look at the issue in a broader perspective.

> Too many of us die at the age of twenty and are buried at eighty.

## What has gone wrong? What has led to the chasm between the children and the seniors?

Things were more defined and simpler in olden days. Be it farming or business, sons used to join their father's occupation. The daughter was supposed to look after the house and children. There was no cut-throat competition and academic pressure like today. Slowly, the women too entered the career fray. Equations changed.

Lifestyle changed. The new set-up brought about new demands. Opportunities widened but so did the rat race. Diminishing joint families, working parents, small flats, different lifestyles, has left hardly any room for old parents in the family.

Vedic society had a wonderful way of gearing humans for old age. They had four divisions of life. Vanaprastha ashram was dedicated to meeting the requirements of old age. This was the time when a person was supposed to leave home and enter the forest to get detached from all material things.

The concept of ageing has changed today. Now who cares about the five-thousand-year old Vedic society? With medicines, fitness regimes, and a will to live longer, they have turned tables. In the past, retirement was regarded as the last phase of life. It was all about reading paper and playing golf. Today, even after retirement, people have so many years to their credit and so much energy left that they don't know how to use it. They are neither too young nor too old. They once again face an identity crisis. Their plight is that of an adolescent who is neither a child nor a grown up. They don't get the feeling of being truly old. Today's older generation still have ambitions left. After all, how much TV can you watch or how much golf can you play? They still aspire to become rich and famous. They know they can still look forward to the likelihood of decades of vitality before becoming truly old. But they are confused as to what they might rightly aspire to in the next phase!

## How old is old?

> "Being old is when you know all the answers but nobody asks you the questions."
>
> **(Anonymous)**

Actually, 'old age' is a relative term. While walking on a crowded road, I see some of the youngsters invariably stepping aside for some of the seniors to pass first as a mark of respect as they have an aura around them. Then there are some elders who are hard to live with. They are crabby and impossible to please. I remember one such gentleman buying vegetables from my vendor and bargaining like crazy. When the irritated vendor refused to sell his veggies to him, the old man started cursing the whole breed of current generation, "Ah, the youth of today! Aren't they horrible?" "Phew! These old people sure get weird sometimes. They waste other people's time because all they have now is 'Time,'" the vendor too muttered under his breath.

Though experiencing old age is different for each individual, there are some indications that make one feel that 'age is catching up.' Nature announces old age with wrinkles and physical decline; the government declares we are old by issuing retirement cheques; children accuse us of being old when there is a difference of opinion; fear of loneliness looms large in old age; and an impending fear of death creeps in.

## How to support the weight of increasing years with ease?

One gets a crash course in dealing with pregnancy or bringing up children. But there are no classes to teach 'How to deal with old age.' Since this book believes in owning responsibility for one's own life, individuals need to assume personal responsibility for how they feel about themselves in old age too. In all fairness, nobody else but we and only we are responsible for our unhappy and unfulfilled old age and only we can do something about it. It's our own personality that matters most. If we believe in ourselves, people will start believing in us. If we have decided to lead a happy old age come what may, nobody can stop us from that.

The moment we understand, appreciate, and accept this simple fact, we have already taken the first step to happy old age. No past age would seem better than the one we are in. And when we change our perspective, a period full of ouches and grouches will turn into one of the most exciting period of our life.

Unhappiness is not necessarily connected to aging. Old age blues are not about aging. As Gene Cohen, a psychiatrist, gerontologist, and director of George Washington University's Centre on Aging, Health, and Humanities says, "It's somebody who has been confronted with all kinds of problems, is losing a sense of control or power, or is dealing with a sense of loss in a maladaptive way." It can be infancy, teenage, adulthood, middle age, or old age. Each stage demands something. Dealing with old age means how well you adjust to declining health, how you take your retirement, how cheerfully you welcome your new role, how well you adapt to the changes that come with age. On the whole, how you add colour to the added years.

> The conscious and unconscious decisions that we make on daily basis, decide how we wish to spend our old age.

## Age gracefully

"Growing old is mandatory; growing up is optional."
(Chili Davis)

If we do not really know how to grow old, we do not really know how to live either. Some people mature with age and get better like old wine. Some, who don't keep pace with time, get rotten with age. Too many people lead small lives. Too many of us die at the age of twenty and are buried at eighty. Such people remain set in their ways and end up being a misfit for the modern times.

Is it possible to triumph over old age, to grow old gracefully? Yes, it is. Grace and wrinkles make an awesome combination. But growing old gracefully does not happen by accident. It takes concentrated effort. One needs to be diligent and persevere. Some enterprising individual has mentioned that there should be two kinds of universities—one for youth and the other for old age. The youth come to learn about sex, life's struggles, and fulfilling ambitions and career. The old return to learn about meditation, death, God, and all things spiritual. The university trains them and disciplines them to graduate to old age with grace. Not a bad idea. Life is a learning process till we die and this is a blueprint for approaching old age in advance.

There are a few principles that can ensure that the growing old experience is a graceful one. We need to understand and apply certain principles much before we come face to face with the inevitable. Some simple and modest changes while we are still young, can bring about a dramatic effect on the quality of life in old age.

## Acknowledge the age

It's important to acknowledge age at any stage of life. Not acknowledging means somewhere something has gone wrong with our growth. But still, "Age is a question of mind over matter, if you don't mind it doesn't matter." It could not be described in better terms than this! All humans go through bodily changes—infancy, childhood; teenage, youth; middle age, and old age. This is the fundamental fact of life. Accept it.

## Start young

Old age is the sum total of all the years that we have spent in youth and middle age. 'As you sow, so shall you reap' the old adage is true in all areas of life, including old age. Those of us who are young must realize that the seeds for a graceful old age are sown while we are young. Our journey from childhood to old age determines the quality of old age. "Most men spend the first half of their lives making the second half miserable," said La Bruyere. (*Sermons from the old Testaments*)

In that case, chances are that we will be replica of the same oldies we despise most. Do not be in a hurry to rush into life. It is like ruining the development of a rose bud by pulling it out prematurely. Each stage is important. Each stage involves certain developmental tasks and optimal time. Handle each stage with care which eventually will help us go through the next stage, or else, we will be endangering our last stage.

If we manage each stage well, we are bound to have a good self-esteem. People with good self-esteem have less hassles being with themselves at any given time. They view difficulties as challenges. They work on their problems with a positive mind. These seniors are a pleasure to be around. Not only do they make themselves happy but they spread happiness all around. The conscious and unconscious decisions that we make on daily basis, decide how we wish to spend our old age. How we behave with our spouse, how we treat the seniors in our house, the way we bring up our children, our eating habits, everything determines our happiness quotient in old age. Choices made by us in the past become our experiences. Experiences shape our personality. And our personality colours our approach to old age. It is in our hands to decide the nature of our old age if we make deliberate efforts to plan for the golden years much early. Old age is like a bank account . . . you withdraw what you've put in. So deposit a lot of feel-good memories and happiness in the young age to cash on in the old age.

## Make yourself financially secure

Prepare for a happy retirement much before you face retirement if you don't want to be bitten by the bug of old-age blues. A healthy bank balance is important to survive the vagaries of old age. There's a correlation between wealth and health at any time of life, especially in old age. Keep some resources for your old age (house, bank balance), instead of giving all to the kids and then be left high and dry, as is mostly the case. Keep your dignity and self-respect intact. Make sure you don't have to face the embarrassment of asking children or friends for financial help in old age.

## Plan for retirement health too

A woman walked up to a little old man rocking in a chair on his porch. "I couldn't help noticing how happy you look," she said. "What's your secret for a long happy life?"

"I smoke three packs of cigarettes a day," he said. "I also drink a case of whiskey a week, eat junk food, and never exercise."

"That's amazing," the woman said. "How old are you?'

"Twenty-six," he said

The problem is that we do not plan for old age that meticulously as we do about other aspects of the future. And those who do, they do not think beyond financial security and a roof. So when the time comes, they are overwhelmed with the issues that they did not anticipate. For example, we need to prepare for the kind of body we want to carry in that phase of life which is almost as long as young age or may be longer. The energy level and fitness counts more when nature announces the arrival of old age. And remember, it does not happen in one day. It takes years of conscious efforts to make it happen. Take good care of your body today, and you will enjoy good health later on. Take your health for granted now and be prepared to face the consequences soon after.

Whatever you eat affects your health, mood, and happiness. Consume alcohol and spoil your health the next day. You tend to get up late with a headache. Drink milk with honey at night and you are ready for the day with a fresh mind. Be careful before you reach your fat forties and things start to get out of hands. Healthy eating habits at young age can ensure lesser problems in old age. Eat wisely and in moderation. Regular exercise, walks, eating habits, taking care of teeth, and a healthy lifestyle are all part of the same equation. Yes, this is one way of ensuring health and happiness. Don't wait till old age to settle and decide what to do. You may not even have the energy to think anymore. If we do not learn this while young, we will waste much of our life pursuing the wrong things, and hate ourselves for it at a later stage. But then it may be late.

## Keep growing—learning is a life-long process

"When I was a young man, I wanted to change the world. I found it was difficult to change the world, so I tried to change my nation. When I found I couldn't change the nation, I began to focus on my town. I couldn't change the town and as an older man, I tried to change my family. Now, as an old man, I realize the only thing I can change is myself and suddenly I realize that if long ago I had changed myself, I could have made an impact on my family. My family and I could have made an impact on our town. Their impact could have changed the nation and I could indeed have changed the world."— *Unknown Author on changing the world.*

Old age is when we stop growing. Old age is when we stop being receptive to change. Old age is when we settle down for rut. Grow up, not old. We talked about paradigm shifts in the earlier chapter. They are must for our growth and happiness. Though we experience a lot of paradigm shifts in different stages of life—childhood, adolescence, and adulthood—we lose flexibility and become rigid in our views and are reluctant to give them up when we grow older. With the result we lose adaptability. We age mentally and physically, and stagnate. Our strategies of life become outdated and stop working further. We fail to keep pace with time. No wonder we become unhappy souls in old age, spreading unhappiness around.

The new opportunities have changed the concept of old age. The market is full of new technologies—Internet, Blackberries, iPods, and what not! There is so much to learn. Life can be interesting even in old age. Everything depends on us. It is never too late to reflect on our choices, to make amendments to live a fulfilling life. We don't need to wait for some drastic event to take place to change our life. We can choose to live a change-oriented life from this moment onwards by bringing awareness to whatever we think or do.

> The problem is that we do not plan for old age that meticulously as we do about other aspects of the future.

## Focus on inner beauty

Ageing is a natural process. Our body cells are being replaced after every seven years. An average body expires ten times when it is seventy years old. Interference can prove detrimental to health. Unless you are in an industry where you need to have good looks, don't tamper with the physical changes that take place in the body. A cosmetic surgery can go wrong. Rather, bring the spring back with the state of your mind. Let the time wrinkle your skin, not your soul. Look inward. Start to focus on inner beauty. It will help you sustain from the inside in old age when your outside starts to fall apart.

Mentally, try to come out of the society that has been a part of your life for so many years. You are no more obliged to be a part of any social group against your wishes. Enjoy the company of people in small doses. You don't need to be dependent on others to feel wanted. Neither do you have to be dependent against your wishes. This is the time when it is best to retire even from social clubs and let others get a chance to enjoy the platform. I am not suggesting you to do this or that. What I mean is that at this stage of life, you have less of compulsions and limitations. You can choose what gives you pleasure.

## Coping with loneliness

Loneliness in old age is our greatest dread. Most people feel isolated after retirement. It brings along with it the feeling of anxiety, abandonment, being uncared for, and insecurity, which leads to depression. Dorothy Donelly says, "Loneliness, a sense of pointlessness, often comes from not having anything to do, or not knowing what to do, or feeling that nothing is worth doing."

Choose to fight, not flight. The horse that is kept in the stable for too long is bound to get the crib-bite. If a man has nothing to do, he would decay like a deserted house. Avoid sleeping too much or watching too much TV. They are nothing but escape routes. Having an agenda in life will help. Involve yourself in something congenial in which you can put your heart. If one has not learnt to empower his thoughts or does not have an outlet for his energies, he will end up being a windsucker.

Most of us will have peaked in our careers by the time we approach old age. All through life, we have tried to rise to the expectations of our dear ones. Now it's time for us to be fair to ourselves. There are no more appointments, project reports, deadlines to be met. We have raised our brood and all are now settled in life. This is the age when we can experiment with different things. Parents, who live their own lives in old age, are happier than those who have nothing to look forward to and live an aimless life. Even the children of those parents who are involved in their lives do better in life. When you don't have an agenda in life, you start interfering in other people's agendas and happiness. Do things you did not get time for in the madness of day-to-day mundane life when you were young. Discover yourself. Develop new hobbies. Do not take your undiscovered talent, inventions, ideas, dreams, hopes, and aspirations with you to the cemetery. Learn new skills—dance, music, chess, computer, read, write, anything . . . If not now, then when?

> Start to focus on inner beauty. It will help you sustain from the inside in old age when your outside starts to fall apart.

Keep smiling. Give happiness to others and get happiness back without asking. Sometimes all it takes is a simple gesture of kindness or thoughtfulness—like giving a bit of your time to another person or a warm hug to someone who is feeling down to make the other person's day. The fragrance always stays in the hand that gives the rose. Cure the loneliness of other lonely people and it will cure your own. On my way to walk, it's a pleasure to see a grey-haired man in his late seventies, sitting in his recliner in the lawn and smiling at passers-by. People are compelled to greet him. Some even stop by to exchange a few pleasantries at times. He is known as 'A happy old man.'

## Be prepared to die

Sounds crude? But this is one reality of life most people avoid facing. As we prepare for a healthy and happy old age, there comes a time when we need to prepare for peaceful death also. Birth and death go hand in hand. Old age is a natural process and death is the only future. No human being is bereft of that. Accept it in all humility. Write your will, think of parting words, and make the moment of death peaceful and also beautiful.

## Avoid a few pitfalls

It will be selfish on our part if we try to stop children from going overseas or out of city to work and settle down at a place convenient to them. It's the requirement of time. One has to accept this fact. The earlier one accepts, the better it is. Rather than having expectations from children and getting disappointed, we better prepare ourselves to fight our own battle. That is why follow these simple rules:

- Walk straight. Let the body be old, but keep the spirit young. Make conscious efforts not to groan while sitting or standing, even if your back or knees hurt.

- Get rid of the clutter, generally collected for old time's sake.

- Do not talk about your health, unless it's good. If you start counting your ailments to friends and relatives, the moment they see you coming, they will change their path. Be thankful to God for the parts of your body that are still functional.

- There are some stress busters such as keeping a pet in the house—a cat, dog, or parrot. These pets keep you company and keep your BP under control. Gardening too stimulates the senses. Exercise, walking, meditation, yoga keep one fit at all ages and help alleviate depression.

- Do not take your safety for granted. Have a safety door and keep the main door chained. Keep valuable items like jewellery in the bank.

- Hire servants only after recommendation from acquaintances and get the police verification done. Find care facilities in your area. There are helplines. Have the numbers fed in your mobiles for emergencies.

## Well, keep your sense of humour alive!

"To every disadvantage, there is a corresponding advantage." (W. Clement Stone)

If it makes you feel better:

When you are old, kidnappers are not very interested in you.

In a hostage situation, you are likely to be released first.

No one expects you to run into a burning building.

People call at 9 p.m. and ask, "Did I wake you?"

Your investment in health insurance is finally beginning to pay off.

Your secrets are safe with your friends because they can't remember them either.

Thank God that you are old!

Things won't change unless we hold the key to a true happy old age in our hands. Enjoy the old age, not just endure. Love yourself, love every stage of life and love others. Let us endeavour to live in such a manner that when we die even the undertaker will be sorry and we can proudly say, "It has been a great journey."

No doubt you want to make required changes to improve the quality of life, or else you wouldn't be holding this book. At the same time, it is not going to be easy as our current beliefs and habits are the results of an old and long conditioning by our parents and society. Do not get impatient. Keep your 'feel happy button' on—no matter what! Get more determined and work harder and smarter to beat it. Work on your strengths. Challenge your conditioning. Your level of self-awareness and understanding of how these factors work, will help you develop new habits. Set small, achievable goals. Small awards give strength and desire to change. Plan out how you are going to work on them. Hold a mirror up and ask yourself every day, "What do I need to look at today?", "Am I doing the right things? Am I sticking to my commitment?", and "What is blocking me?" This is the process that propels real growth and transformation.

A father had taken his son to a pet shop to buy him a puppy for a birthday present. "Have you decided which one you want?" he asked. "Sure!" replied the boy, pointing to one puppy that was wagging his tail enthusiastically. "I want the one with the happy ending."

Make happiness your choice!